LOVE CAN BE FOUND

Harcourt Brace Jovanovich

New York and London

LOVE CAN BE FOUND
A Guide to the Most Desired
and Most Elusive Emotion

Silvano Arieti, M.D., and James A. Arieti, Ph.D.

Library of Congress Cataloging in Publication Data
Arieti, Silvano.
Love can be found. A guide to the most
desired and most elusive emotion.
Includes bibliographical references.
1. Love. I. Arieti, James A., joint author.
II. Title.
BF575.L8A82 ， 152.4 76–27406
ISBN 0–15–154722–X

First edition
B C D E

To our friends
John and Sophie Meth

And we are put on earth a little space,
That we may learn to bear the beams of love . . .
—WILLIAM BLAKE

CONTENTS

PREFACE

Love is sought by everyone, everywhere. It is a constant concern; it is in constant demand. Can it be found? We believe so, if it is sufficiently understood and properly pursued, as we shall indicate in this book.

In spite of a few remarkable contributions, we can definitely state that love has not been the object of much psychological or psychiatric research. Most of what we know about it comes either from our limited private experiences or from the insights that poets, novelists, playwrights, and artists have offered us. With rare exceptions, in the indexes of most psychoanalytic, psychiatric, and psychological books and textbooks we do not find an entry for the word *love*. And even such important cultural media as the *Encyclopaedia Britannica* and the *Columbia Encyclopedia* have no articles about this subject.

We believe that the present team of writers, consisting of a senior author with many years of psychoanalytic and psychotherapeutic practice, and a junior author, a humanist, can be of help to many who seek guidance and no longer want to rely exclusively on improvisation. We have, of course, been inspired by previous contributions, and we have reévaluated the writings of Erich Fromm and Rollo May. Most of what is presented in this book, however, derives from the clinical experience of the senior author and from the dialogue, often animated and unpredictable, that the two authors had about this subject. We hope that we have succeeded somewhat in enlarging our understanding of love, in giving practical advice in terms as clear as possible, and in attempting to formulate a theory to interpret this very human, and yet universal, phenomenon.

Silvano Arieti

James A. Arieti

PART ONE

FIVE TYPES OF LOVE

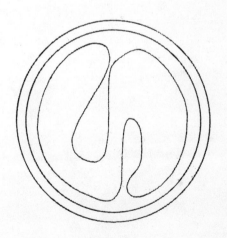

1: THE RAINBOW
OF LOVE

The eminent biologist T. C. Schneirla, who studied all types of animal life from the amoeba to man, reached an amazing conclusion. There is a fundamental activity in all animal forms which manifests itself in one of two forms: approach or withdrawal. When confronted with a stimulus that enhances its survival, the amoeba moves toward the stimulus, almost as if it wanted to caress it. When the stimulus is harmful, the amoeba moves away.

In higher animal species the approach becomes "a seeking or searching for," the withdrawal "an avoiding." In the evolution of the animal scale, we can easily observe that these two fundamental motions are accompanied by increasingly complicated emotions; actually, the emotions generate the motions most of the time. The human infant who sees his mother and experiences the first rudiments of love has a spontaneous urge to approach her. He smiles, extends his arms, wants to grasp her breast, feels happy when he feels the contact of her body. At other times, when he hears a loud noise or sees an unfamiliar face, the baby cries, withdraws his arms, or moves them in a disorganized way, but one which is not grasping.

When human beings have been near to one another for some time, whether they are two, three, or many, they develop two basic emotions or a mixture of the two. One of these two emotions keeps people together and makes them develop reciprocal acceptance, liking, and an attitude of caring. It is the feeling which, in its *highest forms*, reaches the level of love, an intense attraction, a desire for the closest possible approach or union. The other type of emotion keeps people apart, in a state of doubt, alertness, and concern. It is the feeling which, in its *simplest forms*, is called fear. If love already exists, and fear in one of its multiple, often unrecognized forms, sets in, it may transform love into fear. Thus fear, which is a useful protector of life, may degenerate and spoil life's most beautiful promise.

How is fear possible? Does it come about because we do not know what love is, or because we do not understand the essence of our own love? Is the fear caused by the uncertainty of whether love exists in our lives, or by the anxiety that the love we possess and deem so precious may end, even soon, even abruptly? Although we may be satisfied about our work and pleased with the various activities of our life, doubts about personal love haunt many of us almost every day.

Love has always been acknowledged a very complicated emotion. All the attempts to define it throughout the history of our culture, from the philosophers of antiquity to the biologists and psychologists of our era, have ended with controversial results. Love is not an isolated psychological function, or something that ends in the same way as it began; on the contrary, it is an outcome of previous feelings, thoughts, and attitudes which were often unrecognized, undefined, and undeveloped. Moreover, as we shall illustrate in this book, love is not a static emotion. Unless love continues to wax, it tends to wane.

The old tale of love is always new; it can be told again and again in original ways. Those who have voiced their understanding or appreciation of love have throughout the centuries formed a chorus of poets, philosophers, biologists, historians, novelists, composers, singers, painters, sculptors, playwrights, and film makers. Can a book which follows a psychological approach help the individual when he comes to grips with this intricate and powerful phenomenon?

Perhaps there is an answer in the amusing story of a supposed Professor von Von Kochenbach, a German professor who was raised in the Kantian-Hegelian tradition, and lived before Germany became Nazi, militaristic, and materialistic. Professors like von Von Kochenbach are very rare nowadays. One day, von Von Kochenbach saw two doors, one of which, when opened, led directly to love and paradise and the other to an auditorium where a lecture was being given on love and paradise. There was no hesitation on von Von Kochenbach's part. He darted—to hear the lecture.

Do we suggest to our readers that you do what the professor did, that is, read our book, which is somewhat like hearing a lecture, instead of immersing yourself impulsively in a life of love? It may be hard for you to believe, but we do. In our opinion von Von Kochenbach made the right choice. He knew that the sign on the door portending to lead directly to love and paradise was false. There is no easy road to love. Love and paradise are not immediately given or entered. We can only hope to feel love by gaining knowledge of the human heart and mind, and, to quote Plato, by bringing forth what we lack. We must also pursue love by preventing fear from changing love's nature. *A love that is properly pursued is soon to be found.* Many books on the subject have already helped the hesitant and the perplexed. We are not attempting to replace these works, but to offer new points of view and reexamine old conclusions.

SEVEN LOVES

Love may unfold in many ways. In a probably arbitrary fashion we see love in seven dimensions of human existence. Like the rainbow which embraces the sky with seven colors after a rainfall, the rainbow of love can embrace our existence, bestow beauty and pleasure, and renew hope, even when life is difficult or seems desperate and gray.

One of these types of love—the one to which we shall devote our major effort in this book—is love between man and woman, a love which has strong sexual components but goes much beyond sex. Yet we also give careful consideration to the other six types of love, for the understanding of each of them makes clearer the essence of the others. Romantic love in particular has many common, at times almost invisible, roots with the other types of love, and cannot take place or evolve unless it is preceded by them, or unless the person knows of them or becomes capable of experiencing them.

The first of these six nonromantic loves is family love, a love determined originally by a family bond. It is the love that parents have for their children and children for their parents. It may extend to all family members—brothers, sisters, grandparents. The second is love for the other, your "neighbor," or your fellowman. In other words, it may include a special group or the whole humanity. The third is self-love, or the love that a person has for himself. The fourth is love felt for something to be realized, an activity or form of life, a goal to be achieved, a mission to be accomplished, the triumph of an idea or ideal. The fifth type, which is perhaps a variety of the fourth, and which is experienced only by some people, is the love for something that transcends the world of phenomena. Religious people call it love of God, manifested as an ideal to fulfill God's expectations. The seventh love is love for life itself.

Since ancient times these seven types (and many others) have been called loves. And yet they appear so different from one another as to make us doubt whether we are justified to put all of them in the category of love. They must have something in common to deserve the same designation; but whether what they have in common is the essence of love remains to be determined.

Most human beings experience all these seven types of love in various degrees. A considerable number of people experience at least six of them. A few human beings, fortunately an extremely small number, do not experience any love at all. These human beings are in a serious predicament, so much so that they themselves doubt whether their lives are worthwhile. To the extent that we can, we must help them to find some love. Many people do experience love, but their love is distorted by doubts, fears, and other obstacles. Differently from other human tragedies, a life presently without love can be repaired.

In searching for a common denominator of all seven types of love, some argue that love is felt for anything on which our happiness depends. This statement may be true, but with these words we do not define love; we only point out a quality common to the loves known to us. It is true that without a particular love a person would feel deprived and unhappy. The question remains, however, why one's happiness must depend on that particular object of love and not on another one.

In considering romantic love especially, some people define it as that condition in which the happiness of another person is essential to our own. We are faced here with the same incompleteness. Why is the happiness of that particular person essential to our own? The situation may seem easier to understand in relation to parental love. It is evident that the happiness of parents has a great deal to do with that of their children. Parents know that children depend on their love for security and growth. But why parents respond to their children's needs can only ultimately be explained in terms of parental love—a concept not yet clarified.

It could be that many types of love start as, or are elicited by, a need, for instance, the infant's need of being taken care of, or the adult's need to gratify his sexual desire. We shall return to this issue later in this book. However, it is obvious that love goes beyond need; otherwise it would remain a need, perhaps for something essential like oxygen, but would not necessarily become the emotional experience of love.

Other characteristics can be recognized in all types of love. A state of harmony is assumed to exist between the lover and the love object once their union has been achieved. The term *love object*, used by many people, including the present authors, by force of habit and for the sake of common understanding, is not the best designation. The harmony of love does not admit a division into subject and object. Whoever is an object becomes automatically and simultaneously a subject. The loved one is also the lover; the lover is also the loved. This reciprocity exists not only between two persons, but also when one of the partners of love is not a human being. As we shall see later in this book, it may be an idea. A dialogue of love goes on between an idea and the holder of the idea. Although the two lovers interchange roles, they nevertheless maintain their distinct identity. However unequal a man and woman may be, or a parent and a child may be, or a member of a collectivity may be in respect to the other members, the nature of love makes them all equals in the partaking of love, all receivers in giving, all givers in receiving.

This state of harmony we have referred to is implied in some conceptions of love of the classical world. According to the testimony of Aristotle, Hesiod and Parmenides were the first to suggest that love is the force which moves things and keeps them together. Empedocles, too, saw in love the force which keeps together the four elements (fire, water, earth, air). According to him, the kingdom of love is the culminating phase of the cosmic cycle, during which all elements are together in complete harmony.

Another characteristic common to all loves is commitment. A person who experiences love is committed to its attainment, preservation, and growth. Commitment is much more than desire and motivation. It engages one's present as well as future actions for the attainment of what is good not only for the lover but for the love object, too. The loved person or loved ideal is thus not a possession, or something that exists just for the sake of being enjoyed, but also something on account of which one must modify in a significant way the course of one's actions. On the other hand, love is not solely or predominantly commitment; otherwise it would be more appropriately named duty than love.

In the *Symposium*, Plato described another characteristic of love to which we have already referred: longing for what the lover lacks. To love is to miss; it is a desire for a goodness that we do not have. "To love is to bring forth the beautiful, both in body and in soul." Love, however, cannot be defined only as something that we want and miss, and Plato, in what is probably his most beautiful dialogue, did not include only these characteristics in the definition of love. That in any form of love there is a feeling of incompleteness cannot be denied. Love can always grow and improve. Although it is experienced as something good, it promotes movement toward even greater goodness. At first these characteristics seem those of greediness (wanting more and more), but, contrary to what happens in greediness, in love there is also a desire to give more and more, for the improvement of the loved one.

Another characteristic of love is its intensity, what is often called passion. When John loves Mary, if he does not love her passionately, we may be inclined to say that he does not love her at all. If he does not love her madly, we may consider him aloof and indifferent—not the sort of man we would want to marry our sister. If John does not love her wildly, ecstatically, fondly, we may even conclude that he is either taking advantage of her, or is cold, calculating, frigid. If John, in his private moments alone with Mary, were to say, "Mary, I love you reasonably; Mary, I love you moderately; Mary, my love is finite and controllable"—were he to say all these things, and were Mary to ridicule or snub him, we might feel she was entirely justified.

There is no doubt that love is a strong emotion. When we use the expressions *passion* or *being madly in love*, however, we must have a clear understanding of the special meanings given to these words. Such understanding is not usually the case, as we shall see shortly.

What is the physiological mechanism which allows us to love? What is the biological origin of the pleasantness of love? Since the time of Galen it has been known that we experience emotions not with our heart, our blood, our bones, our guts, our glands, but literally with our brain. *We love with our brain.* Even in our present time this notion seems almost unbelievable to some people. What about our sexual organs? For that part of love which consists of sexual functions, we certainly need these organs. However, the pleasure which seems localized in the genital area or other parts of our body is actually experienced in our brain. The central nervous system then projects it peripherally, and we believe that the sensation is occurring in several parts of our body, but especially in the sexual organs.

One of the reasons people are reluctant to see the brain as the physiological organ of emotions and especially of love is the impression that whatever is connected with the brain connotes only thinking, cold reasoning, objective calculations, and cannot include the flame of love, the mystical experience, the fury of anger. A great American neuroanatomist, J. W. Papez, demonstrated that some old parts of the brain experience emotions. Other anatomists and physiologists (Olds and Milner, MacLean) demonstrated that pleasure is experienced in some small central areas of the limbic gyrus. For the purposes of this book it is not necessary to go into anatomical or physiological details. It is important to stress, however, that, as Papez demonstrated, these parts of the brain send irradiations to the cerebral convolutions of the cortex where ideas and intellectual reasoning take place, and give an emotional coloring to these intellectual processes. Papez demonstrated also that these areas of the cerebral cortex, where intellectual processes originate, in their turn send irradiations to the areas where emotions occur. Thus feelings and thoughts converge to form high emotions, including love. Not only do thoughts and ideas participate in the origin and growth of love, but also in transforming its strong physiological, and in some cases orgastic, form into one which may become predominantly or exclusively spiritual.

• • •

LOVE'S GREAT OBSTACLE

How can it be that love, which is admired as the spring of virtue, the source of all that is good and desirable, can become irrational and mad? Can it be that love has two natures?

According to the ancient Greeks, the world is created and sustained by love; but, according to them, it is also destroyed and corrupted by love. These two conceptions of love—the one which sees love as a creative, life-giving force, the other which sees love as a destructive, decaying power—run from almost the beginning of European thought to the present. In Lysias' speech as it is recorded in the *Phaedrus* of Plato; in part of Pausinias' speech in the *Symposium*; in Sappho, in Catullus, in Propertius, in Ovid, we have the beginnings of love seen as a corrupting force. Later, in the Middle Ages, we see Dante's Paolo and Francesca, who were consumed by their love; or we see Abelard, who was made to pay a heavy price for his love. Love and death are often paired together, as in the myth of Tristan and Iseult, taken by Denis de Rougemont as the paradigm of love in the Western world. In modern times we have King Edward VIII, who lost his kingdom for love. Love may distort one's sense of what is most important and less important. When one is shot, wounded (notice the traditional metaphors—when one is wounded by love —an implication that one is no longer whole and healthy) when one is wounded by love, one is willing to do a host of regrettable, even horrible things. One is willing to kill for love, to die for love, to go to war for love. The lover forgets his work, ignores his duties—in short, he makes his beloved more important than everything else in the world.

With Hesiod's *Theogony*, in which love is presented as a divine creative force; with Socrates' speech on love in the *Symposium*, in the magnificent invocation to Lucretius' *De Rerum Natura*, in Venus' roles in Virgil's *Aeneid*, in the Augustinian and Aquinian doctrines of divine love—in all these works we find the rehabilitation of love. Venus, the goddess of love, is transformed from a power of lust—in which role she was responsible for the Trojan War—into a cosmic symbol of order. Thus, although the majority of the great thinkers and of traditions consider love either a noble, constructive sentiment or a principle underlying the harmonious order of the universe, others have seen in it a disruptive force. Even passion is no longer seen as a feeling that has strength and beauty, but as a destructive power, placed at the service of an instinctual urge that sees no obstacle to the attainment of its aim.

It is our contention that in spite of its many components, love has only one basic and positive nature, the nature which starts with the primitive tendency to approach and reaches the stage of embrace and union. The so-called second or negative nature of love is superimposed, is a sort of fear that enters into the most intimate and sublime human relation and deviates its course. The fear may be fear of love itself, in its physical or nonphysical forms, or fear of the loved object. It is thus important that we examine the nature of this fear.

Fear is not the opposite of love, nor as complicated as love. In contrast to love, which is an outcome of previous intricate psychological activities, fear is in many situations the first emotion to be felt and can be defined with less difficulty. It is the emotional reaction to the perception of danger, a danger which can be combated but is preferably avoided.

People fear all sorts of things. They fear disease; they fear driving a car; they fear earthquakes and volcanoes; they fear getting F's on examinations; they fear not being loved by other people. What is present in every fear is the apprehension of harm, harm to one's body, one's emotions, one's personality. One fears the objects which may cause that harm. If one accidentally finds himself in an enclosed place with a lion, he may well experience fear: this fear is based on his knowledge of the nature of lions, that is, that they tend to devour or claw human beings. The same individual might find himself in an enclosed room with a spider and might again experience the emotion of fear. In this case, however, his fear may not be justified, for the spider may be completely harmless. Only an understanding of the nature of the various spiders will tell the person whether or not he has grounds for his fear. If he does not know what the spider is capable of, he will probably fear the spider. This fear will cause him to kill the spider or to run away. If the spider were in fact dangerous, the man's fear will have saved his life and contributed to his survival. If the spider were harmless, the fear will have caused an unpleasant experience and unnecessary actions.

For the animals in the jungle, fear is a message which, if it could be translated into human words, would in some cases suggest "Fight," but in most cases would give the order "Flee, get out, flee as fast as you can." To human beings, too, fear frequently sends a similar message. Of course, the fear of the animal in the jungle has many characteristics different from the fears commonly experienced by people. There are many situations in human life, however, in which a secret, at times unverbalized, or even unconscious, message is heard: "Flee, get out of this situation. Don't be together. This person is not to be loved but feared. Don't trust people." Although these fears are often mixed with an ensemble of images, ideas, and feelings which make them complicated experiences, they can be reduced to the basic core of an elementary fear, to the perception of a threat to the physical or psychological safety of the individual.

Certainly fear is not the only emotion that separates

people or creates distance between them. More complicated feelings bring about a similar effect, for instance,
feelings of anxiety, anger, hostility, hate. Hate is probably
the most complicated of them, and is generally considered
the opposite of love. But if we analyze all these negative
emotions, we recognize that they are built on a foundation
of fear. Fear is the core from which all of them depart and
develop in different ways. Anxiety is a complicated form
of fear; it is fear for something that is going to happen not
in the present but in the future, or fear for something
nebulous or symbolic in its meaning.

Rage, anger, hate, are feelings which help the individual
to fight the source of fear rather than to avoid it. Although
they are often useful in self-defense, they may become
destructive. In this book we shall deal with the core of
these negative emotions, fear; not with fear in itself, but
fear insofar as it is an obstacle to love. Moreover, we shall
not discuss or refer to all types of fear, like fear of ill-
nesses, storms, earthquakes, accidents, and the like, but
only fear of other human beings.

Whether or not fear be proper depends on the nature of
the feared object. However, fear of other human beings is
often based on situations which occurred earlier in the history of our life. Although an original situation in childhood
may have evoked a proper fear, a similar situation in the
present time may not need at all to elicit fear. And yet the
fear may continue. If we know what we should rightly fear,
we are left to love what we should rightly love.

Now, if we consider again these two basic emotions,
love and fear, we are struck by an imposing divergence.
For love we have to look high up, for something still not
completely defined, although strongly positive, something
to which we can add indefinitely. For fear we have to sub-
tract, to descend low into the gamut of possible negative
emotions, and recognize a simple feeling connected only
with the safety of the self. Love points toward the possi-

bility of the zenith of human existence while fear points toward the possibility of its nadir or its annihilation. Fear, as immediate response, quickly brings about the possibility of instant dissolution; love, as a prolonged practice or a style of living, presents itself like an ascending and pleasant journey.

We have mentioned that the number of people who have experienced no love at all is infinitesimally small and that people who have never been afraid are nonexistent. All of us are gripped by fear in some circumstances. Unfortunately these two emotions are often disproportionately distributed in our life: too much fear, too little love. When we pursue love, we must have both the courage to love and the courage to confront fear.

2: FAMILY LOVE

How do we muster the courage to love and the courage to confront fear? The most common and most reliable source of this courage is another love, the love that we receive early in life from our family, especially from our mother and father. Whereas all the other loves have to be pursued, this one is there to be found, as soon as we are born; and it is given to us generously and warmly. It becomes the best prerequisite for the pursuit of all types of love, including the interchange of family love. Parental love provides the security necessary for the unfolding of all loves, and becomes the model imitated by all of them.

We must clarify at once, however, that even the less fortunate people who early in life do not receive any love from their family, or only a minimal amount, are not excluded from the possibility of developing various kinds of love, including the romantic. They have more difficulty in their pursuit and will have to follow a less direct course.

PARENTAL LOVE

The psychoanalyst Therese Benedek wrote that the process of maturation of husband and wife gains new dimensions through parenthood, by the relations they have with the child, and by communicating with each other through the child. Benedek added that the early psychoanalytic theories were wrong in suggesting that the personality is already integrated in adolescence, before the individual becomes a parent. Those of us who agree with Benedek do not, of course, imply that people who do not have children are necessarily arrested in their growth. They generally find other avenues of development; but contrary to what may seem at first, their development is more difficult. A life unburdened by parental responsibilities must find unusual ways to grow and mature.

Parental love is founded on the instinct for survival. This is its biological beginning, but only a beginning for human beings. If it were not so, parental love of humans would be no different from that of the lower species which leave their offspring as soon as they are born or shortly afterward. Parenthood does not consist only of a sexual drive leading to the sexual union, or of the woman's reproductive physiology from the time of conception to childbirth.

When the baby is born, he* is not ready for life outside

* When we use the pronoun he, we follow the prevailing rule of the English language. We do not refer only to the male sex, but to both men and women. When our remarks apply only to one sex, we specify that it is so.

his mother's womb. He depends on his parents much more than the newborn of other species and depends on them for much more than simple nourishment. His prolonged infancy and childhood, which together span 15 to 20 percent of his life, keep him in a lengthy state of physical, emotional, and cognitive immaturity. He has many more needs and requires much more care and love in order to face the environment successfully and to cope with it psychologically. The child does not know the significance of what he perceives and feels. Everything is for him new and marvelous. When he learns the first rudiments of language, he will start to ask his parents, "Why, why?"

What does a mother need as a prerequisite for caring and loving the child? First, she needs emotional security. We do not mean that Victorian security, based on authority, which parents used to have in earlier generations. She needs a more general security, based on the expectancy that life will unfold in the proper way, on the hope that she will be able to fulfill her role of mother, and on the faith that her child will grow up to be a normal and happy person. The father has the same need for security. As Benedek has written, security has a double function: it helps the child, who breathes an atmosphere of security and prospers in such a climate; and it helps the parents to repress fears they may have about the child and about their parental roles. Of course, security requires a certain degree of mental health that, alas, not all parents have. We shall return to this later in the chapter.

The person who is endowed with a feeling of security has a good start toward parental love. The starting point does not coincide with the birth of the child, but may occur during pregnancy, or, if the child is planned, at the time of conception. The parents—mother and father—begin to conceive many dreams and to nourish many hopes about the little human-being-to-be. Thus, parental love is a psychological system that expands around the nucleus provided by the parental instinct.

Soon after the birth, events occur which reinforce the love. These events may be a source of joy even when they are not entirely approved of by the parents. The child seems to imitate the parent in many ways, and the parent sees himself or herself reflected in the child. A sense of continuity is established; as Walter Pater observed, "Through the survival of their children, happy parents are able to think calmly, and with a very practical affection, of a world in which they are to have no direct share." The parents see themselves perpetuated and thus sense that in some way they have achieved a kind of immortality, which, as Plato says, lies at the heart of love.

At first the child imitates the parents in little ways, postures, gestures, expressions; later he imitates the parents in tones of voice, in the use of words and ideas. Still later the child idealizes the parents. Mother and father know everything, explain everything, help in every situation. One could rightly say that this attitude fosters narcissism—that is, high valuation of oneself—on the part of the parent. The parent is pleased with the child's evaluation of him or her and becomes convinced of his or her own worth. Such narcissism, unless it is exaggerated or unnecessarily prolonged, has a beneficial effect. It reinforces the bond of affection between parents and children. For the same reason, it is not inappropriate for parents to foster the narcissism of the child very early in life. It is, in fact, quite common to see young mothers and grandmothers lavishing on little children what appears to friends or acquaintances as excessive admiration. These mothers and grandmothers (fathers and grandfathers, too) seem to be in a state of awesome worship. A little smile, an unexpected act of the baby, are seized upon as signs of genius to come, of extreme sweetness and adorability. A critical observer may wonder whether such an attitude is breeding self-centered tendencies in the child. Actually, this extreme fondness has a beneficial influence; as we have already mentioned, the young human being requires a greater supply of love than the young of other species in order to overcome the greater difficulties, conflicts, and doubts that human life will thrust upon him or her.

The child's growing confidence in himself gives the parents a feeling of fulfillment, for they see themselves achieving one of their life's goals. Thus parental love benefits the mother and the father as it is benefiting the child. It is undeniable, though, that parents and children are not in a relationship of equality. Although parents receive a great deal of satisfaction, they give an immense treasure of affection and physical care that cannot be matched. Only in the broader scope, in the eyes of humanity as a whole, as a generation of children becomes a generation of parents, is the debt of parenthood repaid.

Parental love actually is in some ways a transition from self-love to love for another person. The child, at least before quickening, is experienced by the mother as a part of herself, and love for him is, to a certain extent, still part of love for herself. After quickening, when the mother becomes aware of a new life inside her, her love shifts direction and becomes more and more oriented toward another person. The mother begins to love her child unselfishly. This maternal love, which originates in love for oneself, generally becomes the most altruistic, unselfish kind of love. Mother loves the baby no matter how many and how difficult are the requirements of this love: mother feeds, mother holds, mother fondles, mother cuddles, mother cleans, mother dries, mother talks, mother sings, mother looks, mother smiles, mother moves about. Mother is always there.

Erich Fromm distinguished maternal love from paternal love. According to him, mother's love is bestowed unconditionally, without any strings attached. Father's love is different, for it expects something in exchange. The child must behave well and do well in school to deserve paternal approval and love. Fromm is right in distinguishing these two types of love, but he does not expect us to take him literally or dogmatically. The two types are described in a paradigmatic way, the one being more typical of the mother and the other of the father. Actually, fathers, too, love the child from birth, and after the child has reached a certain age, mothers, too, do not give love unconditionally, but expect a certain type of behavior.

The baby is not able to talk for at least a year, and yet the mother must communicate with him in some way as soon as he is born. No love can grow beyond an initial stage unless there is communication. David Schecter has described the development of the first human bond by referring to John Bowlby's description of primary instinct. According to Bowlby, five instinctual responses are very important in early childhood: "sucking, clinging, following mother visually and with motions, crying, and smiling." These instincts not only insure survival, but communicate love. Although instinctual, says Schecter, they acquire the interpersonal quality necessary for the bond of love. The dialogue of love between mother and child thus is started long before the child's acquisition of language. Mother is aware that the baby does not know the meaning of her words, but, first automatically and then consciously, she communicates with gestures, tone, accent, rhythm, speed, cadence, and melody of her voice. Empathy, a way of feeling in the same way and understanding without the use of words, contributes. It is almost an intuitive understanding, or perhaps an understanding based on little clues, which most all the other adults either do not see or do not interpret correctly. For a long time, only the mother understands these clues. When the child is older, some of these clues can be expressed in words, but the nonverbal part of the communication remains essential. The eyes of mother do not speak but are very eloquent: they smile and reassure. The child looks at them and feels caressed, embraced.

With the passage of time mother and child quickly learn to know each other more and more. It is a knowledge that goes beyond intellectual understanding and involves everything. Mother and child know how the other thinks and feels about matters of common interest. Almost always they know when the other says the truth or when the truth is modified. They know what to expect from each other and what not to expect. When the child is considerably older, they also know what not to know about each other. To know what not to know means to reserve great areas of privacy even in the person you know very well. This implies not only respect for him or for her, it is also a safeguard of his or her individuality. Love, parental too, requires respect for the separateness of the persons who love one another.

THE CHILD'S LOVE

We have discussed the first bond of love, between the mother and the little child, as if it were based only on need or dependency. This was the common understanding of the relation until the mid-fifties. Today many authors, including the writers of this book, also take into account the views recently advanced by the British psychoanalyst John Bowlby. Bowlby believes that the bond between the mother and the child (and occasionally between the grandmother and the child, or the father and the child) is not based on need or dependency but on a special relation that he calls attachment. Attachment develops between the third and sixth month of life and is evident especially after the sixth month. The child clings to the person he is attached to, smiles at her, makes noise when he sees her. Although he cannot talk, he acts as if he considered this person stronger and wiser, a person whose presence brings about reassurance, comfort, and removal of tension. This attachment becomes particularly evident during the second and third years of life. The child prefers to be within the sight of the mother; he feels comfortable when he sees her. While he is playing in the park, he makes little excursions, but always returns to mother. The quality of mother that promotes attachment is her being there, her availability, her thereness. The possibility of seeing her face gives him reassurance.

Bowlby has correlated his observations on human babies with results obtained by other researchers with experimental animals. The well known ethologist Konrad Lorenz found that during the early days of life, birds develop a strong bond to a mother figure (not necessarily the real mother) even if she provides no food. What she has to provide is proximity, being close to the newborn. Harlow demonstrated that a young monkey clung with a sense of attachment to a dummy even though it offered no food, provided it was made of soft material and was comfortable to cling to. Bowlby concluded that in all the species that were studied, food is not a requirement for attachment, but proximity is. Bowlby also believes that attachment is an instinct that has protected animals from predatory species. In animals that live or migrate in groups, females and children are kept in close proximity in the center of the group and the male protectors are at the periphery. Thus we could say that attachment is a precursor of love, or an elementary love that removes fear. Proximity or closeness brings about familiarity; familiarity brings about attachment. Conversely, unfamiliarity may bring about fear. According to Bowlby, the fear does not need to be a fear learned after birth, but inborn fear for the unfamiliar, the new, the startling—a fear that has been transmitted genetically to protect the species. The word *familiar* means friendly, well-known, acquainted with, having an intimate knowledge of—all meanings which portray the origin from the noun *family*. *Unfamiliar* means the opposite, and it is a term to be applied first to what does not pertain to the family.

Bowlby considers this attachment of the child for the mother the basis of all future attachments, that is, of all future loves. The original attachment between the mother and the child makes the child more resistant or less vulnerable to fear. In its turn the state of security reinforces the bond of affection, the expression of love between parent and child. If there is a weak affective bond between the parent and child, insecurity and fears develop and grow, and in their turn the insecurity or state of fear, unless corrected, hinders the strengthening of future love and the development of future loves.

We, the authors of this book, believe that attachment is an important and essential part of filial love and any subsequent love.

However, we believe that proximity alone is not sufficient to maintain indefinitely the positive bond. In the case of filial love, many other requirements—some of which we have already mentioned and some of which we shall describe in this section—are necessary for its retention and full development. If he could talk, the infant would say that he wants something more from mother, not only her being there and touching him. Although he obviously benefits from the embracing proximity of mother and senses the strong attachment, he develops expectations—expectations that he cannot reveal in words, but in other ways, for instance, by crying. When he is hungry, he expects mother's breast to appear. Later the child comes to feel that all things in life result because of the people who take care of him. It is up to the mother to give him the breast, to keep him on her lap, to fondle him. The child learns to see everything as depending on the will or actions of the others, on the people who take care of him. But together with the feeling that everything depends on others, there is also the feeling that people will perform these wonderful actions; the child trusts adults. The baby who cried when he was born, and who cried repeatedly, now smiles. First he smiles at everybody; later at only those people—mother, nurse, father—whom he recognizes as taking care of him. Although the normal child depends on others, he does not eliminate himself as an active participant in this process of love. He learns that his crying, his smiling, his babbling, modify (or even control) the behavior of others. Some psychoanalysts, Silverberg, for instance, believe that the child has a feeling of omnipotence. Certainly, in a nonverbal way, he is aware of playing a very important role among the people he trusts.

At first, of course, the child's feelings of trust are vague and indefinite. The child does not know the word or concept *trust*. Since these feelings of trust cannot be conceived of or expressed in words, they remain at a somewhat primitive level. They are diffuse feelings, sensations, attitudes, and positions of the body; they are a physiological preparation for that nonverbal language which, as we have said, most mothers understand. The child experiences a pleasant anticipation, a feeling of well-being, a trust in people and events to come. This feeling of security, at least in its early stages, corresponds to what Buber, Erikson, and Arieti have, in different contexts, called trust, basic trust, or security; it is a feeling caused by the proximity of human beings from whom good actions or good attitudes are expected.

Later, to retain security, the child expects approval from others. That is, the child expects the important adults in his life to expect something of him; the child trusts that the adults will trust him. There is a reciprocal belief that all is going to be well; parents and child believe that the child will grow into a healthy and mature man or woman. The child perceives the faith of the mother and accepts it, just as he used to accept being fed when he was hungry and being cleaned when he was wet and dirty. He finally absorbs the trust of the adults important in his life, and he trusts himself, too. He becomes more and more self-dependent.

This feeling of trust in oneself and this expectation of a favorable unfolding of life, which is at first limited to the immediate future, is gradually extended to the circumstances of life in general and is finally expanded into a feeling of favorable anticipation toward a distant future. A basic optimism, founded on basic trust, is originated. This feeling of basic trust leads to the feeling of communion, which later embraces other people and even society at large. In this state it is easy for love to grow and for new loves to come into being. Family love cements and unifies. Little unities are formed, not only by virtue of biological kinship, or by a legal contract, but also by love. People are joined together; they are not "they"; "they" becomes "we." Parents and children, referring to members of their own family, say "we." "I" and "you" are two different people, but become "we" by an act of love.

Love between parents and children continues, of course, when the child is older, although the attitude changes. Encouragement and appreciation are useful at any age. The parents' real love is not one which is necessarily connected with the state of dependency of the child. The good parent does not invade the prerogatives of the child; he lets the child become more and more autonomous, and as soon as possible free to make his own choices, even if they are mistakes. Advice from parents to adult children and from adult children to parents is not necessarily to be avoided, provided it is offered as an additional choice. The advice should not be considered a command, and the person who receives it has the prerogative of not following it. When the child is an adult, he does not need his parents as he used to. Love remains, however, though it is a love without need, except the need created by the love itself, the need to be together, to exchange warmth and ideas, and the joy of rejoicing in each other's joy.

We have said earlier that since in the human species childhood is long and complex, parental-filial love is crucially important and has to sustain the child for many years. Even in the primate which is closest to us, the chimpanzee, childhood ends at four years of age; and the chimpanzee has a very long childhood in comparison to other species.

In races immediately preceding that of *Homo sapiens*, in the other so-called hominids, there was already, as Morin and others have described, a primitive organization of society and culture. For the absorption of this developing culture, evolution favored more and more mutations which were characterized by an expansion of the cerebral cortex, until the human size was reached. A circular process was thus established—more culture, more brain —but there was a third ingredient—more love, a love which made survival possible during prolonged childhood, and, with survival, made possible more brain and more culture.

So far we have discussed only love between parents and children, but within a family there is also love between the children for each other. This love between siblings is based on common interests and equality. It is not generally so strong or so stable as the love between parents and children, for in early life there is not so much dependency on the siblings as on the parents. It is also impossible to have absolute equality in the roles that the various children play within the family; there will always be differences in age, character, ability, interest. As a rule, however, in a normal family, when a state of communion has been established between parents and children, a state of love also develops among the children, that brotherly love which is, as we shall see in the following chapter, capable of extending and becoming love for one's neighbor.

THE ATTACK OF FEAR

At this point many readers will certainly wish to remind us that the family picture is not so beautiful, smooth, or sweet as we have depicted. Often the family, which should protect the child from present fears and make him less vulnerable to future fears, is also visited by fear, and is hindered in its ways to promote love.

In which ways do fear and its derivatives enter into the family structure? In some relatively benevolent cases, fear appears in the form of overprotection; parents are scared of life, which looms so difficult; how will the little child manage in this rough world? How will the child, so helpless and frail, encounter the manifold deceptions or face the limitless disappointments of life? In these cases it is fundamental to determine why parents look at life with so much trepidation. Overprotection is sometimes an unconscious way of making the child grow as the parents want him to, that is, it is based on fear of harm to the child because of his own individuality. As Shainess has described, a frequent fear of the mother is shown by her unwillingness to allow the child to test how far he can go in his abilities. Is he able to swim, to roller-skate, to ski, to bicycle, to go on a date? To paraphrase Shainess, as the child is increasingly able to express and cope with his needs, the mother must relinquish her vigilance and her attitude of "knowing it all."

Benedek has remarked that one parental fear, which

fortunately has subsided in the last few decades, concerns the child's sexuality. Parents used to worry about the child who played with his genitals, masturbated, played doctor with other children, petted during dates. Fathers do not exist any more who threaten to cut off the penises of little boys who play with their genitals. A fear of older children's sexuality remains in many families, however, especially when the parents themselves had many insecurities and conflicts in their own sexual life and history. In a very small minority of cases, an unconscious sense of envy on the part of parents who would like to be young again influences their behavior. Benedek states that women who feel positively about their femininity "trust their children since they trust themselves and their own experiences." In the intuitive confidence of their own personalities, they feel they have conveyed to the children their own set of values. Some mothers appear selfish because they do not want to participate in their children's activities. Behind this apparent selfishness there is a profound fear; some mothers, in assuming this passive role, fear that they are incapable, worthless, weak. If they could discuss their feelings, their belief in their own inadequacy could be proved unwarranted. Instead, these women strongly deny the insecurity, fearing lest they be proved undesirable characters, not even good enough to be mothers. Thus their neurosis prevents the demonstration and growth of their love for their children.

A fear which is much more common in mothers than in fathers is the fear of the child's growth. How will he be when he grows up? The mother asks, "Will he depend on me? What will my life be like when he grows up and goes his own way?" These feelings are generally put under the label of "the complex of the empty nest." But if parents have faith in life, they recognize that each stage of life has its beauties and challenges; when the children are grown-up, their parents will discover new horizons.

In some cases, when the pregnancy was not planned, or, if planned, forcibly accepted because it was expected of her, the future mother begins to fear. There is no joyful anticipation at the arrival of the baby, and when quickening occurs, it makes the woman aware of the presence of "an intruder," an intruder now inside her, but soon to be an intruder in her home. The intruder will spoil her body, her beauty; he will become a bundle of demands and needs that she will not be able to fulfill adequately. Similar feelings may occur in the future father, too; he may think that his wife will be less attractive, less desirable sexually, less available, less willing to pay attention to him.

At the time of pregnancy future parents may already attribute ideas and demands to the baby far beyond those of which he is really capable. They may also project into each other attitudes that are not there, such attitudes and feelings as "She will not love the child, will not be a good mother" or "She will love only the child, not me," and "He will not care enough about the child" or "He will care only about the child." Attitudes like these may bring about the psychiatric complications that occur after the birth of the child, and in the worst circumstances even the so-called postpartum psychoses. Frank discussions are helpful in eliminating the fears and apprehensions that future parents have toward each other. We cannot discuss postpartum psychoses or their prevention in depth here, as Arieti has done elsewhere. We just want to say that if a woman has serious doubts and fears concerning her pregnancy, she should seek professional help. The expectant mother should not try to find help in members of her family and especially not in her own mother. The mother (the child's grandmother) may mean well, but is the last person capable of helping her daughter in this very delicate situation.

We have given more consideration to mothers than to fathers; modern fathers, however, have additional difficulties in disclosing and practicing their love for their chil-

dren. Alexander and Margaret Mitscherlich have illustrated this problem very well. The father's role used to be
relatively easy when it was the traditional one of unques-
tioned authority. But now, when fathers are expected to be
as lenient and as flexible as mothers, they often do not
know what to do. As the Mitscherlichs report, many young
people complain of their father's reluctance to enter into
deep discussions with them. This reluctance, often attri-
buted to lack of time in our busy technological world, actually results from insecurity in exercising the paternal role.
The father would rather be a child himself and be guided
by a strong father than to be a hesitant paternal figure.
Deprived of his traditional authority, the father often goes
to the other extreme; he becomes very weak. The child
recognizes this uncertainty as weakness and cannot identify with him. The result is an impairment in the exchange
of emotional attitudes and ideas, especially between
fathers and sons, which may hamper the practice and
growth of love. Some writers have foreseen and described
these recent developments. In Turgenev's novel *Fathers
and Sons*, the relationship between Bazarov and his weak
father becomes one of almost total lack of communication;
to be sure, there is love, but it is a doting, fond love on
both sides.

The role of being a father during the child's formative
years is not biological in nature, but sociocultural, and
therefore it does not have the security or necessity of biological functions. According to the Mitscherlichs, the recent
escape of young people into the world of drugs may be
connected with the weakening of identification with the
father. Undoubtedly the father's position in this contemporary climate of cultural uncertainty and confusion is a
very difficult one; it is certain that the strict authoritarian
role of the past has to be relinquished, but the offering of
concerned guidance, warm advice, and a sense of hopeful
participation must continue.

Reams have been written by psychiatrists and psychologists about abnormal relations between the parents themselves and with their children which do not permit the growth of love. Hostility and callousness are, unfortunately, common among adults, and may cause serious trouble to their children. Trust in what is to come, desire to explore life and find fulfillment, and the attainment of love are threatened in such a climate. We must recognize, however, that feelings of hostility often hide fears. Parents who do not recognize their anxiety feel frustrated, irritable, become angry, have a need to let off steam, and their children are an easy target. Anxiety is fear of life in one, some, or many ways. Parenthood revamps this fear, and parents, at times almost automatically, discharge resentment on the children.

Let us see what happens in these circumstances. As Suttie has illustrated, the child manages to preserve in his heart the lovableness of his mother and father, even when it is difficult to do so. Eventually he can no longer do so. If he expects anger and punishment or indifference and callousness from his parents, his whole attitude toward the world is changed. In fact, mother at first, and later both mother and father, are the representatives of the world.

Martin Buber wrote that there is no I without Thou. Psychologically this means that without others there can be no I, no development of the self. If the relations with the parents are abnormal, or not blessed by a happy state of love, a normal I-Thou relationship cannot exist. The eyes of the mother are no longer caressing or embracing: they are threatening; they see through the child; and what they see is not pleasant. Thus it is better to avoid those eyes. When the situation with the parents is seriously disturbed, not only the parents but any person other than himself tends to be seen by the child as a distressing Thou. Being with others does not originate warmth, friendship, joy of being together, but a latent fear, often experienced as uneasiness and distress. It will be more difficult for the child, even when he is grown up, to muster the courage to love the other, or the courage to confront any fear which derives from the encounter with the other.

Love for siblings is also easily jeopardized in adverse family circumstances. Ancient stories have represented situations opposite to that of brotherly love. Cain killed Abel; there was rivalry between Esau and Jacob, between Joseph and his brothers; terrible controversies arose among the sons of King David. Atreus slaughtered his brother Thyestes' children and fed them to him; Romulus slew Remus. These stories reveal how the ancients, too, were aware of the impact of family enmity, tensions, conflicts, and violence. In these traditional cases, too, one or more children were afraid of the other child or children.

Parents, of course, try to avoid fomenting envy and rivalry among their children, but at times they do not know that they are doing the opposite of what they intend. For instance, they insist that they love all their children equally. This pursuit is a noble one, but impossible to achieve. All loves differ, and parents love different children in different ways. To the extent that they acknowledge these differences, they can prevent the occurrence of envy and rivalry. Difference does not mean fostering special privileges. Many feelings of rivalry are based on the belief of some children that the parents love another child more. Parents should explain to the children why a particular child needs more care or consideration. They must succeed in conveying the feeling to their children that all the varieties of parental love retain fundamental values and are there to be enjoyed and appreciated by each child.

• • •

SPECIAL ATTACHMENTS

The attachment that we have described earlier in this chapter may assume wrong directions which lead not to love but to neuroses. Bowlby describes how separation from a person to whom the child was attached brings about fear, although the separation may not be dangerous in itself. It is an alarming situation, like being in darkness, hearing loud noises, seeing sudden movements or strange people and strange things. These situations, although not inherently dangerous, imply an increased risk of danger. A relatively common condition of excessive separation anxiety in children is school phobia, or fear of going to school. The condition is not caused by fear of the school, but by the fear of being far away from mother. In these cases mother has often used the child as her companion. The child may fear that something dreadful may happen to mother while he is at school and cannot prevent its occurrence. He may also fear that something dreadful may happen to him if mother is not there to protect him. Overdependency, or as Bowlby calls it, anxious attachment, occurs, for instance, when a child clings desperately to mother or to family life. He is afraid to make even little excursions on his own. Some professionals consider these children spoiled or excessively indulged. It seems more probable, however, that these children have become sensitive to the possibility of loss of love by having experienced real separations or threats of abandonment.

A special type attachment that acquires a sexual connotation is what Freud called the Oedipus complex. According to Freud, this attachment is not abnormal and is universal. However, if at a certain age this attachment is not outgrown or resolved, psychological difficulties ensue. In a way somewhat reminiscent of Oedipus in the play by

Sophocles, the little boy, at a certain phase of sexual development, becomes passionately tied to his mother, wants to marry her, has great rivalry for his father, and would like to remove father from his mother's bed. Conversely, the little girl wishes to marry her father and has rivalry for her mother, whom she wants to displace and replace. Incestuous desires and wishes for the death of the parent of the same sex emerge as feelings and ideas which are strongly felt and strongly feared. It is at this point that the little child experiences a great fear of the punishing parents. The boy is afraid of being castrated (actually he is afraid that his penis will be cut, not his testicles), and the little girl is afraid of losing her mother's love. Freud adds that the girl may feel already castrated and this feeling enhances in her a feeling of inferiority. Freud believed that eventually the child gives up his loved parent as a love object. The parents who are experienced as inhibiting and forbidding adults are transformed and become part of the child's psyche. They become his superego. If this Oedipus complex is not solved, however, various fears, like fear of castration, punishment, or incest, will remain and will prevent a normal unfolding of the functions of the personality, including the capacity to love. Not only did Freud consider the Oedipal situation universal, but he also felt that culture begins with the prohibition of the oldest desires which stem from the Oedipus complex, including incest.

There is no doubt that incest is a form of attachment that has been forbidden since prehistoric times. According to the Hobbesian view, without the constraints of society and law, man would engage in these forbidden actions; it is civilization rather than nature which prevents incest. The Talmud presents a parallel view: man left to himself would not set any limits on his sexual behavior; adultery, homosexuality, and incest would all take place if there were not the laws revealed at Sinai.

Incest appears to be almost universally rejected among mankind, as much in tribes separated by vast expanses of ocean as by sophisticated and technologically developed societies. There are a few tribes attested to by anthropologists where incest is practiced, though it is condemned; and a still smaller number where incest is actually encouraged (see Flugel). Animals freely commit incest, and its prohibition seems to exist only among human beings. One might almost suppose that one distinguishing mark between men and animals is the absence of incest among men.

According to some anthropologists, incest leads to a deterioration in interpersonal bonds: where brothers compete for the same sister or where son and father are rivals for the favors of the mother, hostility will always breed and discord inevitably erupt. The family or the clan, thus weakened within itself, will stir up strife. According to this view, incest leads to a disintegration of the tribe.

St. Augustine, in his *On Christian Education*, propounds a theory of incest which is very similar to the anthropological argument just cited. He starts at the other side of the question and argues that society will be much stronger if there are prohibitions against incest. He begins by accepting the Aristotelian premise that man is *by nature* an animal which lives in a society. Since society is generated by the associations of individuals, a society will be strong when there are many and diverse bonds between citizens. If a man marries his sister, then many of the familial associations are occupied by the same individuals and fewer people are brought into a network of relationships. In the case of brother and sister marrying, they also occupy the bond of man and wife; their children will be siblings as well as cousins; the parents will be uncles and aunts as well as parents; and so on. The family will be a tight unit by itself and the society will not be strengthened by an increase in associational bonds. Therefore, since society is formed by these associational bonds, and since these bonds will not exist in any large number, society will be weakened to the point where it can no longer cohere. Although facilitated by physical proximity and remnants of childhood feelings, incest has roots also in fear, in fear of forming attachment to strangers, in the fear which causes love to turn where there is little risk—toward those whose natures are less mysterious, for they are most similar to one's own. This fear, like others, can be overcome at the outset, as it is in the case of most of humanity, by developing love for people outside of one's family, namely, love for one's neighbor, the subject taken up in the next chapter.

OTHER OBSTACLES

The conditions that make the development of family love difficult are not exclusively psychological in nature but are also sociological and political. The so-called nuclear family seems to hinder family love and to cause disturbances of various kinds. The nuclear family consists of a small number of people, generally parents and children, without grandparents, uncles, aunts, or cousins to be seen because they live far away. The members of the nuclear family live in little space, generally a small apartment without garden, compete for room, for material and for emotional possession, and are ridden by hostility and rivalry. Each of the members of the family becomes the target of the others and is less willing to accept the others. There are no relatives to neutralize the attitudes of the parents if they are neurotic and offer poor parenthood to the children. The home is often greatly deprived of educational, vocational, and religious values. The nuclear family is destructive not only for the children but also for the parents, and especially for the woman of the house. The destructive forces of interpersonal conflicts come to the fore with more violence, and are not diluted or softened by a large number of contacts or activities. It is beyond the purpose of this book to examine whether the nuclear family is a product of industrial society, as some sociologists affirm, or of more general processes, generally included under the heading of modernization. Since the large family of old that welcomed relatives and close friends at any time is not likely to return, society has to devise substitutes, such as closer ties among neighbors, a subject which we take up in the next chapter.

3: LOVE FOR
THE OTHER

ENLARGING THE CIRCLE OF LOVE

Although the infant cries before he smiles, and experiences
pain before pleasure, even in the act of birth itself, he does
not begin his life with fear of others. He smiles at everybody. It is only when he develops attachment and love for
his mother that he smiles only at her, and a little later at
other familiar people, too, but not at strangers. Thus he
soon learns to distinguish the familiar from the unfamiliar,
people who bring comfort from those who do not. It
seems that this division was necessary in evolution for the
emergence of the bond of love. With his overt behavior
the child discloses that automatically and unconsciously
he has formed two categories. In one category are the people who love the child and whom he loves, the persons

who are close to him and protect him. In the other category are the others, indistinct and vague.

The others are not necessarily people who hurt. As a matter of fact, family love, which at first made necessary this division, becomes necessary for overcoming this division itself, and for extending one's love, transformed in various ways, to the others who are not family members. In the previous chapter we have seen that the acceptance of the first Thou, the mother, is the best prerequisite for the acceptance of any other. But who is the other? The other, in our present discussion, is generally referred to as the neighbor.

"Love thy neighbor as thyself." The sense of these biblical words seems first to indicate that a man should not love everyone, but only his neighbor, he who is in close physical proximity and who has common interests and desires. The term *neighbor* is especially effective, for a neighbor is one we see every day, on whom we are likely to call if we need help, whether the help be protection from a storm or fire or intruders or thieves. Need which cannot be satisfied without external help is probably the beginning of the system of neighborly love. But need, as we have seen in Chapter 1, is not love; it is only the starting point of love.

It is easy to understand how geographical proximity and smallness of size facilitated the bond of neighborly love, an extension of family love. In small communities or clans, as they developed among the prehuman species of hominids or even in primitive groups of our species *Homo sapiens*, a kind of love existed like that which members of a family have toward one another. We know that the Eskimos living today experience strong affection and concern for the members of their whole community. In some tribes, according to anthropologists, immediate members of the family were not recognized as a necessary part of the family's hierarchy. In some, the father was not recognized; in others, the uncle was the leader, but the uncle, although assuming paternal functions, was a member of a "brotherhood" that included the whole tribe. It may be, then, that brotherly or neighborly love is more ancient than that existing in the family. Tribes became larger, as human relations intensified and diversified, and eventually became cities and countries.

In large groups, physical proximity can no longer be maintained and the simultaneous sharing of significant experiences becomes increasingly limited. Mutual work and often collective activities still exist but become regimented, mechanized, perfunctory, or ritual. Whereas love for one's family develops spontaneously, "love for the neighbor" in a large society becomes possible only as an act of will.

From ancient times on, people have varied as to the collectivity to be included in the circle of neighborly love. Anthropologists tell us that whereas members of a tribe loved one another, they even practiced cannibalism toward members of an enemy tribe. Fellow citizens, members of the same religion or ethnic group, are often included in a circle of love, but others are excluded. At times exclusion becomes a matter of policy, in order to breed solidarity within a group, by distinguishing "us" and "them." Only the greatest voices, like those of Isaiah and Jesus, rose to stir men toward a universal love for each other.

The message "Love thy neighbor as thyself" is not restricted to the neighbor in a literal sense, but is aimed at including the whole of mankind. When we feel spiritually close to another, he becomes a neighbor in our heart. We all share the same mortality and the knowledge of such mortality. We are all in this together, for better or for worse. The "neighbor" in this conception becomes any person other than yourself. Yourself and the other become equal, as far as your love is concerned. Whereas you bestow family love on the members of your family, this new love of yours must embrace the family of man. Every human being becomes a brother or a sister to you.

If you love any person over whom you cannot pass the judgment whether he deserves to be loved or not on his individual merit, your love acquires a special meaning. In this type of love the special characteristics of the loved person are not important. What is important is *your loving attitude*. The loved person must only belong to the plurality whom you are inclined to love, whether it is your clan or the whole of mankind. Moreover, as we shall see shortly, this loving attitude has special characteristics, dissimilar from those of other types of love. Even if we take into account these distinctions, is it really possible to love your neighbor, no matter who he is? The founder of psychoanalysis says no. In *Civilization and Its Discontents*, Sigmund Freud wrote that love is a valuable thing and must not be thrown away. Love imposes obligations and sacrifices. The loved person must be worthy of love. Freud wrote that it is understandable for one to love a person who is like himself because he loves himself in that person. It is understandable, too, to love a person who is better than oneself or a person who happens to be the son of a friend. But, Freud adds, if there are no specific reasons for loving, to love will be difficult and will be an injustice to those who truly deserve to be loved. Freud asked whether one should love another simply because that other is a denizen of the earth, like an insect or an earthworm or a grass snake. Unlike the Old Testament, which urges the Jews to love the stranger because they themselves were once strangers and hated in the land of Egypt, Freud stated, "Not merely is this stranger on the whole not worthy of love, but, to be honest, I must confess he has more claim to my hostility, even to my hatred. He does not seem to have the least trace of love for me, does not show me the slightest consideration."

For Freud, any type of love, including the love for the neighbor, is libidinal in origins, a derivation, substitution, or sublimation of sexual love. Since Freud takes erotic love, especially in its sexual manifestation, as the prototype of love, he focuses on the "love object." It is certainly true that the person you love romantically is very important as a result of your choice. You have chosen him or her because of certain qualities that he or she has.* As we have already mentioned, in loving one's neighbor it is the loving attitude that counts, one's willingness to include all the members of the collectivity. This type of love has no sexual components or very minor ones. It is a functional system, which among others includes the following feelings and concepts: "My neighbor is my peer. I have respect and concern for him; I feel committed to the safeguard of his rights, uniqueness, and personal dignity. Although each one of us has his own individuality, we are all equal in the framework of these feelings and ideas. I expect my neighbor to feel for me, as I feel for him. He is potentially my friend. That means that I am potentially ready to assume some responsibility for him." The concept of potentiality is important here. Obviously we cannot be responsible for everything or for everybody. The potentiality becomes actuality when some special circumstances arise. Everyone has access to our sense of responsibility, to our willingness to help and care. Our participation will be dictated by our feelings, judgments, and commitments.

Freud's greatness cannot be doubted, especially when we consider that he was the one who uncovered many secret mechanisms of the human psyche, particularly the unconscious and the symbolic processes. We must recog-

---

* Many animals do not choose the mate. For the male dog any female dog would do, provided she is in heat. There is no choice there, not even a choice of universal character including all female dogs in heat, but instinctual coercion. Choice is a human prerogative.

nize, however, that Freud focused on what was primitive and irrational in man, or on what is derivative of what he later called the death instinct. Perhaps a latent but pervading pessimism directed Freud to stress the negative sides of humanity. And of course he could find support for his ideas in the fact that the human being often follows his primitive urges, the ways of the id and of the archaic ego.

Other writers, including the authors of this book, stress that man, just because he is man and not another animal species, has the possibility of overcoming what is primitive in him; and in the majority of cases the folk of the earth succeed in doing that. Some readers may think that we describe man not as he is but as he ought to be. But the knowledge of "oughtness," of a way that will remove us from the primitive animal nature, is part of how we are, part of being human. Whatever wisdom and knowledge, whatever meaning in our emotions and in our relations with others we are able to pursue and achieve can be ascribed to this quality in man that outgrows the primitive.

In defining love for the other we made a reference to potential friendship. Within the large group of the "others" we make choices; we select some for whom we have a special affinity or communality of ideas and interests or with whom we can have fun and play. They become our friends. Mankind honors and respects friendship. A person who abounds in material goods, but has no friends, feels poor indeed. Love for the other, which may be extended to the whole of humanity, becomes even more desirable and even more obtainable if one feels that mankind can provide him with friends.

Freud is not the only thinker who has found difficulty in enlarging the circle of neighborly love. It is realistic to expect that if love is extended to many people, there is a loss in intensity. Aristotle, who writes about friendship in books 8 and 9 of his *Nicomachean Ethics*, says that since it is impossible to know many people well, friends are necessarily few in number. In fact, there exists an inverse relation: the greater the number of friends, the weaker the friendships. According to the philosopher Max Scheler, the value of love decreases when love is given to a larger number of people, for instance, when it is extended beyond the family boundaries to include the fatherland or humanity. According to Scheler, it is wrong to think that there is a hierarchy of love in which love for the family is inferior to love for the fatherland, and love for the fatherland in turn inferior to love for humanity. Quite different is the conception of love of another German philosopher, Ludwig Feuerbach. According to him, love is one, but can be progressively extended, from the sexual object to the child, from the child to the parents, then to the family, tribe, and people in general. This extension results from the multiplication of reciprocal dependence among individuals and institutions. The final stage of this progression is love for humanity as a complex whole—the highest object and the moral ideal.

Two thousand years before Feuerbach, Plato had conceived of a hierarchy of love. In the *Symposium*, Plato has his character Socrates describe the progression of love from the physical to the spiritual. For Plato, love begins with the love of physical beauties, first in individuals and then in nature, but develops into the love of ideas and theories. For Plato, love always reached upward, toward the spiritual; for Feuerbach, love reached outward, toward the rest of humanity.

In the large framework of love for the other, we must consider special relations, such as that toward a political leader, such as the chief of a country. The concept of authority causes a disagreeable resonance in many people today, especially young people, because the concept generally connotes legal power, the right to command others. We must remember, however, that *authority* comes from the Latin *auctoritas*, which, in turn, comes from the verb *augere* (to make things grow, to increase, to produce).

Thus, in its original meaning, authority is the "capacity to make things grow." For human beings, it means sharing knowledge or offering constructive examples to others. The person with genuine authority is authoritative, not authoritarian; he does not have the power to intimidate others. By imparting knowledge or understanding to others he increases, not decreases, their range of action.

Whether the chief of state should be loved or not is a problem that many writers have pursued. Machiavelli gave full consideration to the question of whether it is better for the prince to be loved or feared. He concluded that it is better for the prince to be both loved and feared, but if he can elicit only one of the two feelings, fear is preferable. Machiavelli explains that love is maintained by a bond of obligation that is often broken by human beings, who are generally evil. On the other hand, fear is maintained by the constant threat of punishment. We cannot accept Machiavelli's reasoning, not because a Renaissance prince is necessarily different from our chief of state, but because we cannot accept Machiavelli's moral philosophy. His main concern is the increase and preservation of the ruler's power, not the improvement of man, and he teaches how it is possible for a prince to retain his power by exploiting either fear or the greed and selfishness of the masses. In a democratic form of government, the aim is to help the greatest number of people to live by law and to help create a national form of love for the neighbor.

FEAR OF THE OTHER

As we have already mentioned, Freud's pessimism about love for the neighbor at first seems plausible. Often the least your neighbors can do against you is to gossip. And often the least feeling of anger that one has for his neighbors stems from the desire to be as they are, to live up to the Joneses. These feelings do not originate from a loving attitude, but from the fear that one's neighbor can live better than we do, a competitive attitude. "To live better than we do" in history often came to mean to be more powerful than we are. If the neighbor is more powerful, we become afraid of him, or we feel we should be afraid. We, too, want to be powerful. Thus the race toward power for power's sake originates.

In *Civilization and Its Discontents*, Freud again reminds us that rather than expect love from one's neighbor, one should expect adherence to the ancient motto *Homo homini lupus*. Man is a wolf to the other man, ready to attack and devour him. In this saying, however, a distinction is implicitly made between being a man and being a wolf, as well as the inference that man could act like a man but instead he acts like a wolf. If we study history and sociology, we can easily convince ourselves that people have chosen to act even worse than wolves, by committing barbarous acts against other ethnic, religious, and national groups. In the book *The Will to Be Human*, one of us (1972) has examined the significance of these developments at a socio-political-national-international level. We shall not discuss this vast topic in this book.

Dealing with the problem at a personal level, we wish to illustrate first of all that in most instances it is fear of the others that does not permit the development of a positive feeling for people, and least of all of friendship and love. The others whom we fear do not need to be enemies of our country, but they may be persons who belong to our ethnic, religious, or national group, even our next-door neighbors, any person other than ourselves. This fear is to be found most of the time not in the history of our national or ethnic group but in the history of our life, or of our family. It has great connections with those problems, discussed in the previous chapter, which handicapped or prevented the development of family love. The person who early in life had the adverse experiences that we have described has no feeling of communion or basic trust for the other. He has made a big and unjustified generalization; he has extended to people outside of his family the feelings he once had for the members of his family. He feels that the others will reject him if he does not behave properly, will humiliate him if he does not live up to their expectations. In many instances the parents and the other family members did not intend to inflict this insecurity on the person. As a matter of fact, from adolescence on, the individual may have more feelings of insecurity with people who are not members of his own family. He has learned to live in the family group and to recognize its good qualities. But when he is facing the large outside world, he experiences an interpersonal fear. In many instances the fear is difficult to recognize, and requires a great deal of introspection or psychotherapy in order to reach the level of awareness.

In most cases, fear of people does not manifest itself as anticipation of danger to one's physical safety but as an expectation of being made to feel inferior, inadequate, less than the other. There is also the fear of showing one's inadequacy and inferiority to others. In other words, what is feared is an attack on one's self-image, on one's sense of one's own worth as a human being.

This fear often arises as uneasiness in being with people, even with people one knows. The individual is not able to talk or act freely and remains on guard; words or ideas do not come easily. In many instances he remains an observer or watcher of himself. When the fear is stronger, he feels blocked, embarrassed, even ashamed. In some other cases the situation is worse. What is felt between the individual and the others is not just uneasiness but a barrier. The individual is afraid to expose himself lest he be ridiculed and shamed. He is not even able to admit to himself what he experiences. If he were asked to discuss the matter, he would deny being afraid of his fellow man. In many other cases he is aware of these feelings, but is reluctant to reveal them to others. At most he admits he is shy. Yet what does it mean to be shy? According to Webster's dictionary, *shyness* means: (1) the quality of being easily frightened or startled, timid; (2) the state of being ill at ease with other people, extremely self-conscious, bashful; (3) the condition of showing distrust or caution. All these feelings portray a fundamental feeling: fear of the other.

Fear also encourages withdrawal: the person who is afraid of being rejected often quits before facing the possibility of being rejected. He does not accept offers of friendship, avoids going to parties and other gatherings. In some cases, the person is not just afraid of being rejected, but also of being accepted, because once accepted he will be recognized as inadequate, and will be eventually rejected after having first been accepted, which is worse. Sometimes there is even a fear of being accepted and of being found adequate, for such acceptance and recognition involves commitment and having to live up to it. Moreover, by keeping a distance from the others, by limiting his contacts, the person suffering interpersonal fear may induce the others to misunderstand him. The neighbor may not recognize that the person is shy and may believe that he is haughty, cocky, condescending, and unwilling to be a friend. Thus the other may show an unjustifiedly distrustful attitude, which in turn seems to prove the validity of the fear. The fear is thus reinforced in a vicious circle.

When the fearful man looks at another, or sees another looking at him, he often cannot sustain the glance for a long time and looks away. He avoids making what psychiatrists call "eye contact." The French philosopher Jean-Paul Sartre has given great consideration to eye contact.

He attributes to every human being a feeling of discomfort when another person looks at him. According to Sartre, even though the other may not be aggressive or reproaching, the individual feels dispossessed. Sartre thus believes that one's encounter with the other is lived as a conflict or state of anxiety. But when there is a sense of communion or basic trust, when there is an absence of anxiety and fear, the individual does not have the feeling of being invaded and dispossessed by the glance of others. As we mentioned in Chapter 2, the embracing glance of the good mother remains the prototype of the human glance and predisposes the person to accept glances, no matter from whom they come. The glance is often a welcome gift and an exchange of pleasant feelings. The eyes that complete the face's smile accept the image of the other into them, provide a bond of acceptance, and show the joy of reciprocal acceptance. Only the person suffering from interpersonal fear resents being looked at, feels that he is watched, found at fault, inept and shameful.

The person who experiences interpersonal fear has great difficulty in loving—how can one love somebody of whom he is afraid? He develops psychological mechanisms with which he tries to protect himself, but these make his condition worse. In a considerable number of instances the person becomes almost insensitive in order to protect himself from his fear; he becomes detached, removed from his own feelings, introverted, and in extreme cases that come to the attention of the psychiatrist, withdrawn and shut-in upon himself. Such feelings were often already manifested in childhood. Although children are not able to express them, their dreams reveal the significance of them. A young patient, who started therapy at the age of twenty-four, reported the following dream, which he remembered having had when he was from eight to ten years old. "My family lived on the edge of the town, on the top of a cliff. The members of my family were forbidden to enter the town, and yet they had to get food. I felt I had to go to the town to get food. When I was there, soldiers discovered who I was. They chased me. I ran back to my home, but members of my family had closed the door because they were afraid of the soldiers. I had the choice of surrendering or jumping off the cliff. I jumped off the cliff. I woke up in terror."

This nightmare reveals the intensity of the fear that the patient experienced in childhood. As with all dreams, the content is symbolic but the symbols are metaphors that are easy to understand. The patient's family is without food (love) and is already excluded by the large community. They live at the edge of a cliff, that is, on the brink of emotional disaster. The patient had experienced his home as a cold, very unpleasant place to be in. There was no spiritual food there, no love. In the dream he feels that if he does something drastic, heroic, he will obtain love. Thus he challenges the danger, goes to the city, and faces the others. But the others have undergone a dramatic transformation brought about by the feeling of estrangement and fear. The neighbors are no longer neighbors, physically or psychologically. They have become enemy soldiers, persons in uniform and ready to fight. The patient wants to go back home, but now he is ousted from his home, too. He has lost forever family love and neighborly love. He must choose between a life without love or death. He chooses death. The dream is an intense representation of the patient's inner anguish. The terror was real and already experienced at an early age. It could not be expressed in words, but could be represented in dream form.

This example of very pronounced love deprivation is reported here in order to facilitate the understanding of less marked and much more common cases that involve a large number of people. Fear of the other determines in the individual either a state of anxiety or withdrawal with detachment. In either case, of course, there will be increased difficulty in obtaining or experiencing neighborly love and the loves which derive from it.

In numerous cases the person who suffers deeply from interpersonal fear and is not capable of withdrawing or becoming insensitive resorts to the use of alcohol or drugs like marijuana and hashish. There is no need for us to point out how dangerous these methods are, for the amount of alcohol or drug needed to remove fear always increases as the person becomes used to their effects.

Very differently, fear will sometimes induce the person to ingratiate himself with others, to please and placate them. He will try to obtain their approval, acceptance, and love at any cost. But his efforts soon fail; the others grow accustomed to the special treatment and continue to expect submission and subservience from him. The individual will eventually resent having to pay so high a price for approval and neighborly love and will decide that it is better not to be loved.

Fear of the other may also lead to an attitude of suspiciousness. We are not referring to that excessive suspiciousness which, in a small number, develops into a paranoid type of illness. We refer to a distrustful attitude, which makes one believe that other people will not help in times of need, that they have no understanding, and that they nourish hostility.

PREPARING TO LOVE THE OTHER

If we do not feel ready to pursue neighborly love what can we do? There are at least three ways to be followed. The first consists of evaluating accurately whether or not the other is to be feared. The second is a form of self-analysis that aims at discovering our inner dispositions to fear the other. The third is an attitude of meeting the other with open heart and authenticity. In the rest of this chapter we shall examine each of these three recommendations.

First of all, we must ask ourselves whether hostility really exists in the intentions or actions of others. In a considerable number of cases we shall come to recognize that what we considered hostility was the strangeness of the others, and our inability to understand their different ways. When we are facing people whom we do not know or who seem different from us, we tend to respond like the six-month-old baby, who, as we described at the beginning of this chapter, does not smile anymore at unfamiliar persons. It is not a result of chance that the word *hostility* comes from the Latin *hostis*, a word that has two meanings because of the original confusion between two connotations: *hostis* means both enemy and foreigner or stranger. If we get to know the unusual or strange ways of the other, we shall be able in many cases to discover that they are not meant to be or to appear hostile. By no means do we want to convey the impression that hostility does not exist. Hostility exists, and is caused by fear, as well, of course, as by lust, greed, possessiveness, power-seeking, and vindictiveness. What can one do when others try to hurt one? Can one sincerely love his enemies? In Proverbs 25:21 it is written, "If thine enemy be hungry, give him bread to eat; and if he be thirsty, give him water to drink." Can one really live in accordance with this precept?

In psychotherapy, patients often realize that acts of hostility directed toward them are not necessarily attacks against them, but are manifestations of the limitations and conflicts of the hostile persons. This understanding enables the patient not to hate these persons, and eventually makes friendship with them possible. For instance, a nasty individual tries to insult you, to belittle you with arrogant, obnoxious remarks. If you understand that the basic reason he does so is to aggrandize himself, to hide from you and from himself his terrible feeling of inferiority, you can still defend yourself, but without hateful and revengeful tactics.

Though we acknowledge the existence of greed, possessiveness, and desire for power, we do not need to consider them as instincts natural to man or as parts of the death instinct described by Freud. Rage and aggression originated in the animal kingdom as mechanisms to protect the species from natural enemies and to provide it with nourishment; in man, however, these mechanisms most of the time changed their objectives. They became possessiveness, and desire to increase one's power by decreasing or removing completely the power of the other. These tendencies, of course, are incompatible with love for one's fellow man. In a circular manner, lack of love for one's neighbor generates aggressive tendencies toward him. In some cases, strange as it may seem, aggressiveness takes the place of love. It is a way of relating to the other, not the way of *Homo sapiens* but of *lupus*.

We must be fully cognizant of the existence of these unfortunate tendencies in some men. We must remember, however, that the *lupi* are and have been a minority. Unfortunately they have often been in powerful positions or in positions in which they could increase their power. They are the emperors, the dictators, the tyrants, bandits, murderers. We should not minimize their evil deeds, the anguish and suffering that they have caused to millions. On the other hand, when we evaluate the whole of mankind, we must recognize that the majority of people have overcome and outgrown whatever primitive and sadistic trends existed in them. They are willing to extend a hand to their fellow man, and to convey a message of friendliness and love. Had this not been the case, the human race would by now be extinct. Even in periods of brutality the countless little good deeds of people have bestowed a great amount of goodness upon human life. Sooner or later, the psychopaths, criminals, and vicious leaders have been defeated. The kindliness of the masses have more than counterbalanced the so-called death instinct and have proved wrong the dictum *homo homini lupus.*

Unless there is evidence of malevolence, it is better for a person to assume that his neighbor wishes him well, and is not after his money, blood, or seeking to destroy his reputation or his human dignity. Of course, by trusting, one runs the risk of gullibility and of being taken advantage of by unscrupulous people. But all in all, gullibility is better than allowing one's life to be permeated by an everlasting feeling of distrust and suspiciousness. Gullibility is not, of course, a virtue: alertness, knowledge, and openness of mind soon uncover slyness and cunning.

In by far the majority of cases, the person who wants to pursue love for the other must persuade himself not so much that no danger comes from the other, but that in most instances the fear of the other is something he himself fabricates. This is a most important point. The person must become aware of those anxiety-provoking developments stemming from one's early life history that we have described in a previous section of this chapter. The individual who introspects, remembers, and connects his past with his present is able to reach unsuspected conclusions and to lose fear of the other. Only when the fear is extreme, or the connections with the past and the meanings given to these connections have become unconscious, is the help of a therapist necessary.

If these reflections are successful, the person will soon come to the realization that his need for the other is greater than his fear of him. He may even become more aware of his state of loneliness. Now that he is ready to find a remedy to loneliness, he allows himself to experience it in all its unpleasant aspects. He who feels no longer afraid but lonely feels the need for love for the other and from the other. In a short period of time he will open up to others. He will not put up fronts. Fronts are necessary shields or armor when one is afraid. A person who is not afraid is not reticent about disclosing how he really is. He will show his authenticity. He has learned that when he made pragmatic accommodations to his fear, he could even show to the others a self which is the opposite of what he really is. If he trusts his authenticity, his spontaneous warmth and his social nature will come forth. He will conclude that the others will see in him the essential sameness of themselves. On the other hand, to expect to be accepted warmly by everybody is utopian. Undoubtedly there will be some people who will not welcome him with open arms, people imbued with fears, prejudices, or even preferences which are rooted in unconscious motives. In many instances these people are behind him in the process of human growth. The readiness for a warm social encounter will be there, provided something else is also available, self-love—the topic of the next chapter.

4: SELF-LOVE

LOVING OTHERS AND ONESELF

Can we love ourselves as we love others? Can we be both the lover and the beloved in a single reflexive relationship? Can we divide ourselves into subject and object?

It is evidently impossible to love ourselves as we would love a sweetheart. Were we to accept the Freudian model of love, in which all types of love have their origin in sexual desire, loving oneself would be an abnormality. It would be a narcissistic love, an outcome either of advanced psychological regression or of fixation in the first stage of development. It is apparent that by self-love we mean something entirely different, with no sexual implication.

The search for an understanding of self-love is not new. Aristotle called it φιλαυτία (filautia), by which term he meant the desire to appropriate for oneself the good and the beautiful. Thomas Aquinas wrote that the individual loves himself when he loves his spiritual nature. Max Scheler stated that self-love is not different from love for others and has nothing to do with selfishness.

To love oneself means first of all to accept oneself and therefore value the image that one has of himself. Accepting oneself does not mean that one should consider himself perfect, wanting to be just as he is. Self-love is also a striving to make one come closer to what he believes he ought to be. Recognizing one's limitations and shortcomings does not mean rejecting one's self, but making attempts to overcome what can be overcome and to accept what cannot be changed. Loving oneself does not require one to be selfish but to engage oneself in one's own unfolding.

As Fromm has aptly described, if self-love is not so easily accepted as a concept—as an acceptable love—it is because it is considered by many the opposite of loving others. If one loves himself too much, how can he love his neighbor too?

The New Testament says, "Love thy neighbor as thyself." It does not say, "Love thy neighbor *instead* of thyself." In some theological circles the saying has been interpreted, "Love thy neighbor more than thyself." Do more for him than you do for yourself. If, therefore, you should find yourself in a lifeboat with another person, when your ship has been wrecked, and if there is but enough water for one person, a Christian is expected to give the water to the other person. According to the Talmud, if the first person is in some way responsible for the safety of the second—if, say, the first is a parent of the second or a member of the crew and the second a passenger, the first should certainly continue with his responsibilities and give the other the water. Otherwise, he ought to realize that his blood is just as red as the other's, that his life is just as precious to God.

He must love himself at least as much as the other. And if there is no legal or moral responsibility for the other, some equitable solution will have to be reached. Fortunately, such circumstances wherein one must save the other instead of oneself are extremely rare.

According to Freud, there is an antithesis between loving oneself and loving others. Love consists of a certain fixed amount of libido; if the libido is invested in others, it cannot be invested in oneself, just as if one gives money to others, there is less for oneself. Freud does not see love as more like beauty than like money; no matter how many people enjoy the beauty of a painting or a landscape, the beauty is not diminished. The father of psychoanalysis believed, as a consequence, that some withdraw their love from external objects into themselves and become narcissistic. According to Freud, the example of one who completely withdraws his libido from others and invests all of it in himself is the schizophrenic—a point of view denied by other authors.

How can a person practice self-love? Again we must say that first of all he must become aware of whether self-fear exists in him. Self-fear is seldom recognized and consequently seldom overcome. In the second place a person must practice self-exploration. Self-exploration, however, although important, is not enough. Such procedures as meditation, introspection, analysis, are useful when they activate one toward the third step, that of self-cultivation, or even self-creation. We shall examine these three steps in succession although it will appear evident that they are related.

•　•　•

FEAR OF THE SELF

Fear of the self manifests itself in several ways. One way is the fear of knowing oneself. The Socratic dictum "Know thyself" is not observed because the individual is afraid of knowing. This fear of knowing stems from the desire to hide a part of oneself. Whatever is hidden or repressed can be recaptured by psychoanalytic treatment, but often the individual who is afraid of knowing himself is also afraid of such treatment. The fear is of seeing, of discovering unpleasant truths about oneself. But why should someone be afraid of himself? What can he discover that is so bad? A vague fear is often rationalized. Some will say, for instance, that they fear discovering criminal instincts in themselves; they recognize their hostile feelings and suspect worse. Vindictive fantasies, however, do not make a person a criminal. If a person is a criminal, he knows it; he does not need to discover it from deep within. Others, believing they have certain inclinations, contemplate with horror discovering themselves to be homosexuals. Apart from the unjustified prejudice against homosexuality, after puberty people know whether they are homosexual or not; no deep knowledge of oneself is necessary. Nor do some homosexual leanings make a person homosexual. If a person has latent homosexuality, a condition much rarer than once assumed, he should be happy to find out about it, because the latency may bring about other troubles, much more to be avoided than homosexuality itself.

The truth is that reasons given to justify the fear of knowing oneself are rationalizations. People with this fear have, of course, little self-esteem and a low self-image. One thinks that if he is so bad, he may perform terrible actions, or he may not be able to do what is expected of him; he is inadequate, incapable, inept, undesirable, unlovable, and so on. People will not want to be with him, will not want to be his friends, his partner in love, his co-worker, his neighbor. It is obvious that fear of oneself goes together with fear of others, which we discussed in the previous chapter. This poor self-image is the result of early un-healthy conflicts with members of the family in childhood, as we discussed in Chapter 2. When there was no state of communion, when even those closest to oneself, mother and father, were not experienced as givers of love, warmth, and approval, the child developed a negative self-image. When the parents were not lavish in positive appraisals of the child, the child may have exaggerated the weight of parental discontent, and for this reason felt unloved, un-approved. From this moment the child developed ways of compensating for or remedying his own self-image. One way of compensating is to expect magnificent accomplish-ments of oneself, to expect to become a great individual deserving glory or rewards; another way is to help needy others beyond human capacities. The need to compensate for one's suspected defects in this way is what Karen Horney has called the "tyranny of the shoulds." But these "shoulds," since they are excessively onerous, can only end in defeat. When the individual realizes that he cannot reach glory, that he cannot fulfill his inner dictates, he ends up by feeling even more inferior, and he may even hate himself. The more he is displeased with himself, the more he needs to compensate and the more he is defeated—and a vicious circle is generated.

But the man who has "hitched his wagon to a star" and failed is not inferior, is not worthless. He must reacquire respect for himself. In a vain attempt to remedy the situa-tion, he may take inappropriate actions. On the one hand, he may give vent to his inner resentment by finding inno-cent targets, by becoming hostile and vindictive. On the other hand, he may become self-effacing, and feel that he does not deserve anything good. When this latter feeling is accompanied by a general feeling of not having lived up to the promise of life, he suffers deep depression, and resignation sets in. Why try? The battle of life, the constant struggle is lost. At times, in utter desperation, one has a secret wish for a *deus ex machina*, a mythical mother, a Santa Claus, to rescue him from his hopeless, helpless misery. Such rescues, however, are rare, and fruitless unless accompanied by love.

Erich Fromm states that a person who does not love himself cannot love others. Fromm is right. We add that the converse is also true: *a person who has received no love or has not loved others cannot love himself.* Love always forms a circular process. Even in self-love, which seems only a self-reflected emotion, a circle of love is implied. Each type of love is maintained and sustained by the others. When a person is defective in self-love, we must ask what went wrong in the relations he had with others. He must then be helped to reacquire a feeling of trust and relatedness.

If one's self-fear is very pronounced or if one is very depressed or very hostile, he must seek professional help. In many less serious cases of self-fear and inadequate self-esteem, however, one may help himself. When he catches himself being too harsh with himself, or making too heavy demands on himself, and despairing about his ability to do what he would like to do, he should ask himself, "How would my best friend feel if I do not do this; would he be angry? And how would I feel if my best friend could not do this; would I be angry?" Most normally the answer will be no. The self-doubter will not need to invoke the image of the best friend more than a few times, nor would it be advisable. Only in the beginning of practicing self-love should he ask the questions, in order to remind himself that self-love is connected with love of others. He must try to think, too, of what he did well in life, his accomplishments. If he is a doctor, he should remember how many patients he cured; if a lawyer, how many clients in distress he helped; if a mailman, how many letters of good news he delivered; if a teacher, how many people he opened to the marvels of the world; if a shoemaker, how many people he enabled to walk comfortably. The neurotic, tyrannical "shoulds" will be eclipsed by true accomplishments. However, the best way to go to the root of the problem is to clarify the origin of the low self-esteem, as we have described in Chapters 2 and 3.

SELF-EXPLORATION

Self-exploration requires repeated inquiries about oneself and one's life. The self-explorer must acquire knowledge of the events, especially in childhood, that molded his existence, as well as of the basic patterns of action that confer a given, often rigid, quality to his life. He must also ask himself, "What person am I now, and what person do I want to be in the future?" In other words, in the process of self-exploration he must come out with a sufficiently clear definition of his own identity. All the roles that he has assumed in the past must not only converge and coalesce but integrate in a way which will reflect the core of himself. Erik Erikson wrote that unless identity is achieved in adolescence, the young human being is in danger of falling into a state of role diffusion, or simultaneous maintenance of many roles without a definite and enduring personality.

Although it is true that identity-seeking is a problem that pertains particularly to adolescence, exploration of one's identity is desirable at any age. Who am I and what meaning do I want to give to my life? What is the main goal I want to pursue? Is my aim in life to pursue happiness? Do I know what I mean by happiness? Is the search for a meaning of my life more important than happiness? Each person must try to answer these basic questions and must do so in his own ways. Only then will he be able to make life designs which are in agreement with his inner self.

SELF-GROWTH AND SELF-CULTIVATION

The human being is born into the world ready to grow both physically and psychologically. By the time he has reached his twentieth year, his physical growth has ended; but his psychological growth may continue for as long as he lives. It is in this sense that the French philosopher Lapassade wrote that the human being is always unfinished, *inachevé*. He is always exposed to new situations and to his own attempts to understand them and to develop feelings for them. In doing that, he is always in a state of becoming, of perennial formation. We can metaphorically say that in cultivating himself he is building or improving his own home, the home that he loves because it is his. The person who is narcissistically involved with himself and believes he is perfect or better than the others does not really love or help himself. He would be in a static position except that the human being cannot remain static. The end of growth means the beginning of decay.

Differently from other animal species, the human being has a nervous system capable of absorbing a seemingly endless amount of ideas, feelings, and attitudes. The person who cares for himself considers the new and evaluates whether it could be integrated with what is already part of his life. Some people believe that it is too late for them to improve themselves, that they are too old, that too many brain cells have been used or too much energy has been consumed. These notions are wrong both from a neurophysiological and from a psychological point of view. Our brains consist of billions of neurons. The interconnections of these neurons are astronomic in number, beyond the possibility of calculation. Many neurologists and physiologists have said that the human being uses only a small part of his cerebral cortex. Learning is at its peak in childhood and adolescence, but at a lower rate it continues for the rest of life, if there is physical health and the proper psychological disposition.

Another point has to be clarified. The individual who practices self-love cannot take for granted that he has a definite and limited potentiality for something, a potentiality that he must actualize. He is not like an acorn, which can become an oak but is also forced to become an oak or nothing else. A person may have a certain talent, offered to him by nature, and certain opportunities, offered to him by the environment, but he must also choose to cultivate the talent and use the opportunities. He is able to select those directions which are in agreement with his desires or with the meaning he gives his life. The symbolic functions of the human being, like ideas and words, are capable of infinite combinations and expansions. Consequently, even a person who practices self-love, self-growth, and self-exploration must accept the fact that to a certain extent he will remain unpredictable and unkown to himself. Growth and unpredictability increase the complexity of the person, but it is a complexity that is accompanied by internal organization, harmony, self-acceptance, and faith in oneself and one's inner worth. Again we return to mother, to that faith that she had in us when we were babies. Her faith, which was an act of love, is now our faith, our self-love. Let us make a point clear, however. It is our faith not because we accept it and incorporate it passively. We did so in our early childhood. Now it is a faith that, although it retains the warmth of mother's faith, is the outcome of our self-growth and self-cultivation.

5: LOVE FOR WORK

WORK, COMMON AND UNCOMMON

Love for an activity and love for the outcome of that activity are included in what we call love for work. If I am a carpenter, I may love making a chair, and I may love the chair itself once it is made because I was the one who made it. Whereas in previous chapters we discussed love directed toward human beings (family members, neighbors, oneself), we refer now to a love for something, like a chair, which is not human. The difference is greater in appearance than in substance. The making of a chair is a human act, and the chair itself is to be used or admired by some human beings. We do not do things for themselves. Whether we do them for utilitarian, aesthetic, or economic reasons, we include them in the great parameter of human life and heritage. In the structure of our society the most impelling reason for working is to earn a living, not love for work as an activity or for the result of the work. It is unfortunate that many people work exclusively in order to provide for themselves economically. When there is only this motivation, people may consider work a punishment, the heritage of Adam, condemned to work after he was chased from the Garden of Eden.

It is, perhaps, easy for us to see how a gardener, a carpenter, a physician, a teacher, a nurse, a captain of a ship, an architect, could derive satisfaction and love his work. But what about the millions who toil and sweat in the factories, in the coal mines, repeating hour after hour the same motions while working on a single part of a product, which they will never see in its final state, and about whose ultimate destination or use they have nothing to say? It is not difficult to see how the alienation described by Marx and his followers can take place. When a man is compelled to work without being able to decide on the amount and outcome of his work, he becomes disenchanted and alienated. Society and industry should do everything in their power to revitalize the interest and respect for work which once existed in the artisans of Western Europe and which still exists today in the privileged occupations (teachers, artists, physicians, and the like). Some experiments with variations in the assembly line hold great promise, but, of course, much more remains to be done.

The degree of civilization of a society is to a large extent measured by the many ways in which work done by the masses is organized, so that it is less consuming of human energy, more rewarding, and has an accrual of collateral qualities and benefits that make it desirable.

There are some positive aspects in practically every kind of work that give a feeling of pleasure to the people involved, even when the workers do not particularly like the required activity or care about the product they make. Whether the work is the sublime, almost supernatural work of creating art or of unlocking the secrets of nature, or whether it is a routine activity already done thousands and thousands of times by many, many others, the individual may develop what we have called a feeling of "hereness." The feeling the individual has is that there now exists something that he made that was not here before. It is almost a miracle. If the individual is religious, he may believe that God, having made the worker in His image, has imparted to him, even if in only an infinitesimal degree, His power to make what was not here before. (It is, incidentally, in this sense that a poet and God were called "maker," for they engage in creative actions.) If the worker is not religious, he can reaffirm his faith in his human abilities. The feeling of hereness comes not only from creating visible objects; the ideas which a teacher has imparted to his pupil are now "here," present in the pupil's mind.

A second positive feature is the feeling of accomplishment, which is related to but not identical with the feeling of hereness. Whereas the feeling of hereness focuses on what we have done in the world, the feeling of accomplishment focuses on how we feel inside when we feel fulfilled by what we have accomplished. The most humble job, as well as the most unusual and complicated, can give a feeling of accomplishment. A job well done, whether it represents a menial activity or a highly intellectual effort, means to have created more order in the human world and to have been useful.

A third reason for experiencing love for work derives from the fact that work makes us belong more intimately to the social group of which we are part. One works together with other people and does something that will benefit other people, too. A typical example of collective work is the medieval cathedral built by thousands of different men, at times over a period lasting a few centuries. Here the end was to be a building devoted to God, and it was to be the common product of an entire city, whose citizens were motivated by a common purpose. The common, collective aim need not be a beautiful cathedral admired throughout posterity; it may be the work of running a hospital, a school, a home for the aged. Collective work does not need to have a lofty aim in order to be extremely important. For instance, the man who works on a road so that thousands can reach their destination, the street cleaner who keeps up the standards of our hygienic life, deserve the feeling of doing something valuable to the collectivity.

It is easy to understand how much creative people like Dante, Michelangelo, Newton, Bach, and Einstein loved their work. The work of these geniuses, and of many more of similar rank, shaped and reshaped culture. We must accept the fact that such a level of creativity is reached by only a handful of people in any generation. Yet most of us must also accept that our work is meaningful in human society even if it does not reach such peaks. In fact, it is capable of giving us a sense of fulfillment, and has some qualities in common with high creative work. The creative person is an explorer of the unknown and by virtue of his work he will make us see, hear, or use what until then was not seen, heard, or used. The creative person roams in the realm of the infinite to enlarge what is finite, and to make possible whatever was impossible until then. Thus creativity is a special type of the phenomenon of hereness which we have described in the average man. Both the creative genius and the average worker bring to hereness something that was not here before. With both common work and creative work, something that was not real is made real; a mere possibility has been changed into actuality.

We must also be aware that struggle, constant effort, and at times anguish are experienced by the creative person, too, not only by the factory worker. As a matter of fact, the creative worker may often experience anxiety and disappointments greater than those of the common man. Could even a Michelangelo be sure that he could transform a block of marble into the Pietà or the statue of Moses? From biographies of great men we have learned of the toil and tears, the doubts, discouragement, sacrifices, disbelief or misunderstanding from others, and poverty that they had to endure and to overcome in the pursuit of creativity. Love for creativity requires a commitment and a struggle that at times reach unsuspected intensity. In short, both creative and average work require a loving attitude that renews endurance and dedication.

Those who can derive no satisfaction from their work must find other endeavors to pursue; they may seek political and religious activities, almost anything which can become a repository of dedication, hope, and love. Many people develop a tremendous zeal for entities that appear greater than themselves: their country, their faith, a philanthropy, the triumph of a cause or an idea. The gamut of possible activities and pursuits open to even the average individual is immense. Finally, among the activities that human beings enjoy, we must include hobbies, games, and entertainment of various kinds. It is not the purpose of this book to describe them. They are available to everybody. The person who loves work must love entertainment, too, for the pleasure that he may derive from it as well as for the promotion of camaraderie and social warmth.

FEAR OF WORK

Many people cannot experience any joy in activities of any kind. We shall not deal here with difficulties caused by social, economic, and political factors—areas that are very important but beyond our competence. We shall deal with psychological difficulties, which—as we have described in reference to other types of love—stem from fear. We wish to point out that even the alienation that Marx described hides an underlying fear. The alienated worker says to himself, at times in an unconscious, unverbalized way, "I am afraid that I am wasting my life, that my determination, incentive, motivation have been crushed. What am I? Nothing but a tool to be used and thrown away." The person who is merely bored with his work, who says that he would like to change jobs, that he is tired of doing what he is doing, experiences in a less dramatic way a few of the feelings of the alienated worker. The fear of work often is simply fear of being exploited, but not in every case by the employer or the government. It is the fear of working in order to satisfy the whims of the wife or husband, or the children, parents, or, indeed, even to please society.

A most common fear concerns the outcome of what a person is doing. He fears that the outcome, whether it pertains to a work of art, a small business, or a family, will reveal how inadequate he is. Fear of the outcome has many origins, which are all related. The person who is fearful finds support in his life history; whatever he did in the past did not lead to fulfillment. The work he did was trivial or poorly executed; any new idea was actually a rehash of an old one. Upon examining his past more deeply, this type of person discovers that he nourished grandiose aims, that he had an idealized image of himself.

Many of those who fear the result of their work entertained in their youth the hope of being creative in art or science; and a certain number of them do have moderate talent in one field or another. Their talent might sooner or later have found suitable outlets if they had properly cultivated it, but their grandiose self-images did not permit development. For instance, some may explain that they did not go to school to learn the basic techniques because "teachers stunt creativity, are concerned with technique, not with the content or spirit of the work. They teach one to do only what the public wants, and don't care about true art. Sooner or later you become a disciple, an epigone, or one who prostitutes himself to the crowd." These words may have a ring of truth in some cases, but not in the majority. Even the great masters had teachers. Technique, learning, discipline, should not be confused with imitation or conformism. If their grandiose self-image did not distort the views of these people, they would realize the value of discipline.

Others attribute to themselves the quality of being excellent businessmen, executives, politicians, or the like. While such people live in the fantasized glory of tomorrow, they accomplish nothing today. Often they make real sacrifices for the sake of their glorious aims; and what is worse, they impose sacrifices on other people, especially their families. For example, even though there may be small children to be taken care of, they insist that their wives go to work. They will thus be able to spend the day waiting for the moment of inspiration to come. Later, as they realize that their accomplishments are small in comparison with their expectations, these people grow increasingly discontented. Eventually, they rationalize their difficulties; in some cases they blame their families; in others they feel it is society that does not permit their self-fulfillment. They offer bits of political, sociological, or psychological evidence that allegedly show how they cannot be their "real" selves. Or they may become involved in utopian or outlandish philosophical systems, and may argue that their problems would be solved if these systems were accepted by a society that has so far remained deaf. As their lack of accomplishment makes their positions increasingly untenable, some of them feel forced to accept jobs that their contemporaries have already outgrown; and again they feel resentful and discontented. Soon they stop working, and their fear of beginning something new is greater than before. A grandiose aim or exaggerated self-image may thus lead to psychological disaster. Horney rightly pointed out that this idealized image, which leads to a vain search for glory, is a substitute for a lack of self-confidence. The lack of self-confidence derives from a basic anxiety that originated in childhood when, as a child, the person was unable to live up to the image he felt was necessary to win parental approval and love.

A European-born patient, a most competent physician, used to suffer recurrent periods of depression and feelings of inadequacy, with definite suicidal notions and occasional attacks of rage. Although extremely competent as a physician, he disliked medical work. After a while his work became less satisfactory, he lost patients, and was almost ready to give up on life. He felt tremendously frustrated, dissatisfied, unwilling to continue his work.

He soon disclosed that he had not wanted to be a physician, but had aspirations of being a great writer. Since his adolescence he had devoted several hours every day to writing fiction and poetry; but the publishers had rejected all his works. He did have considerable talent for writing, but since he was involved with his medical work, he could not develop it. Still, he had daydreams of winning the Nobel Prize for literature.

It happened that when he was four, his parents sent him to live with friends in a distant city. The parents felt persecuted by the Fascists, and wanted to be sure that their child was safe. The family reunited later, but little Henry felt he had been punished. Mother and especially father always stimulated him to become a "great man," always commented on his intelligence, and incited in him great ambitions. Because Henry had to divide himself between his literary and medical work, he never achieved those high goals to which he aspired. Still he felt that only if he became great would he keep his parents' love, or the loves that later replaced parental love. Until the conflict was solved, Henry continued to suffer frustrations and hatred for the medical profession.

Sometimes the parents of the child who develops a grandiose self-image have unwittingly conveyed the idea to the child that he will be a worthwhile individual only if he lives up to their hopes. Many parents, of course, do believe that their child will prove to be a great person. Their transmission of this belief is generally not only untraumatic but is actually helpful to the child when it is an expression of love and hope and if being a great person does not mean winning the Nobel Prize but excelling in human qualities. In other words, the normal mother is inclined to believe that her child will be a great person because she loves him, and does not expect greatness or excellence in exchange for her love. The desire to fulfill the real or supposed parental expectations becomes a neurotic urge only when it is interpreted by the child as a requirement for obtaining approval or love. If this neurosis is not treated, the person will feel unable to tolerate his work.

It is characteristic of man to visualize high goals for himself. It is not necessarily neurotic for a mother or for the growing child to have aspirations that will later be recognized as grandiose. Having high aspirations is a stimulus toward progress. The fact that, say, only one in 100,000 persons will live up to his hopes does not make such high goals automatically neurotic in 99,999 persons. Greatness inspires everyone, especially young people. Teachers often portray the heroes of the past in an idealistic light in order to elicit in the child the desire to emulate them. The non-neurotic man eventually realizes that he may grow even if he is not creative or great. The effort he might have spent in vain projects he devotes toward the growth of the self.

This growth will require that he accept work as an important part of life and that he develop fondness for his own activities.

It is not necessary to build a grandiose image in order to come to feelings of inferiority, self-effacement, and despair, although the sequence of events we have just described is more frequent than generally supposed. There are some people who feel inferior even without having conceived a grandiose image, and on account of this feeling of inferiority are afraid of themselves, principally of their own work. This feeling is experienced as a sense of powerlessness, and this powerlessness invades every activity of life. The person believes he is incapable; he is afraid of initiating actions or works. Alfred Adler was the first psychologist to study these feelings of inferiority. According to him, the feeling generally originates in organic inferiority. Bodily malformation, weakness, or disease give the child a feeling of inferiority very early in life. Adler realized, however, that organic inferiority, although it is important, is only one cause of the feeling. Children also feel inferior because they are treated like inferiors by adults, and because they feel that they cannot face the difficulties of the world without the help of adults. They see themselves as small, weak, helpless, unable to cope with the challenges of existence. Adverse relations between parents and children, as we described in Chapter 2, often perpetuate and deepen the feeling of inferiority.

A moderate feeling of dissatisfaction about one's own work or activities has a different origin and is often experienced by people, outstanding in their own fields, whom no one would suspect of having such feelings. Leonardo da Vinci and the great Italian poet Leopardi are two who felt inferior despite the greatness of their achievements. The feeling is based on the discrepancy which exists between the way a man sees himself and the way his mental processes make him see what he could be. Man always falls short of what he can conjecture, and he can always conceive of a situation better than the one in which he finds himself. This discrepancy is caused by the height that the symbolic process of his mental functions can reach.

Everyone, whether endowed with unusual or ordinary powers, must accept the difference between the way he is and the way he thinks he ought to be. He should always try to grow, but no matter how much he grows, he will always be *inachevé*.

We must stress again that the greatest preventive for these fears and negative self-evaluations is mother's love. The feeling of being worthwhile and accepted, which comes from the mother first in the form of unconditional love and later in the form of basic trust, better than anything else prepares the child to overcome either the acute shock or, more often, the painfully slow realization of the discrepancy between the way he is and the way he used to envision himself. One might, in certain circumstances, be helped by a transcendental love, as we shall examine in the next chapter.

6: LOVE OF GOD

Having accepted the limitations of humanity, both religious and nonreligious men retain an intense craving for what is not limited or relative. They seek what will substitute clarity and certainty for mystery, perfection for imperfection, goodness for evil, justice for injustice, and love for hate. In other words, the religious person craves for God, and the nonreligious, who cannot conceive a supreme personal deity, craves for a state of absolute perfection which, although alien to our human status, is not alien to our conceptions and feelings. The religious person calls this craving "love of God"; the nonreligious, "seeking the absolute." In our twentieth century both positions are deemed acceptable, in spite of the fact that people who adhere to one position are reluctant to accept that of the other group.

In this chapter we shall consider the positions of these

two groups, not how they differ, but how they are able, in their yearning for the most desirable good, the highest value, and the greatest type of love, to have many things in common. We shall call this yearning "love of God," even if it does not imply a personal God, but only the ideal of the absolute. Thus it is not necessary to believe in God in order to understand the arguments of this chapter. If the nonreligious reader can conceive of an absolute standard which exists apart from human considerations, he may legitimately deliberate upon the nature of love for this entity.

The pagan Stoic philosopher Epictetus wrote (Epictetus 1.16):

> Great is God, who has given us such implements with
> which we shall cultivate the earth; great is God, who
> has given us hands, the power of swallowing, a stomach,
> imperceptible growth, and the power of breathing
> while we sleep.

Epictetus' hymn to God suggests that God is responsible for all the good which exists on earth. The argument that the orderliness and beauty of the world result from the operation of a deity is generally known as "the argument from design" and has been used for thousands of years to prove the existence of God. According to this argument, the orderly change of the seasons, the majesty of nature, in which every creature seems to be taken care of, the excellence of anatomical features—all these fine touches of nature prove the existence of a superintending divinity. In Plato, the divinity was called a demiurge, and was responsible for, among other things, the placement of all the organs of the body in as perfect a way as possible.

If all men accepted this argument from design, man's love for God would be simply the love of an inferior for a superior being, a love founded on gratitude. We humans would love God because He is responsible for our existence, for the fact that we have digestive systems and hands, and can breathe even while we sleep. The love in this case would be very much like the love which a child has for his parents, a love which is largely based on the innumerable unrepayable kindnesses the child has received.

Aristotle said, "It would be absurd for a man to love God." Despite the great philosopher's remark, it has been a principle of Western religions that God is to be loved. When Aristotle made his declaration, he had in mind a God so far removed from human concerns that there was little one could love with his heart. For Aristotle, God is a first cause, an unmoved power who begins the chain of cause and effect which leads to the formation of the universe. In a modern sense, one might think of the primordial explosion which, according to some physicists, began the ever outward expansion of the universe. The Aristotelian God has thus been deprived of many pagan attributes, but has been reduced to a first cause whose nature is hardly lovable.

Even those who admit they are religious, and who maintain that they love God with all their heart and all their might, will agree that they do not have a thorough and consummate knowledge of God. Indeed, the exact nature of God is one of those mysteries that have always plagued and will always plague man. The question is, then, how it may be possible to love something whose nature is obscure. Certainly no one would say he loved a woman he had never met, and it would be foolish infatuation if he maintained love for her without first having studied and examined her character. Yet man is commanded to love God even without a full—indeed, often with only a very meager—understanding of his divine nature. And if we cannot know God, how can we love Him, for surely it is even more difficult to love something than to know it.

God, however, is a special case, and where He is concerned, it may be that love begins where knowledge ends. When we posit a God, we posit as his attribute perfection, and this perfection includes absolute goodness, knowledge, and love. Because we human beings are finite, we are unable to comprehend absolute goodness, knowledge, and love, but because we know these to be good, we know that their perfect forms can only be best. Thus, even though we cannot understand the full and complete nature of God, we can understand that it will be lovable. An evil man, one who does not know the value of knowledge and goodness and love, would not love God, for he would not know that God's attributes are to be loved. (It does not therefore follow, though, that a man who does not love God is evil, for even if a man recognizes the values of goodness, knowledge, and love, he might not accept God's existence. Such a man, however, *could* love God.)

Kant (*Critique of Practical Reason*, ch. 3) says that to love God, as an inclination, is impossible, for God is not an object of the senses. It is, perhaps, true that one cannot love God as one would love a sweetheart, and yet as the goodness of any possible sweetheart is less than the goodness of God, one's love for God ought to be greater, at least insofar as love can spring from the intellect. For Kant, loving God means obeying his commandments, a notion which also presupposes a God who cares enough about the human race to give them moral obligations. In this way, love is an activity, and involves the carrying out of obligations believed to be God's law. Love of God is manifested, according to Kant, by acting in accordance with God's wishes.

Descartes wrote toward the end of his Third Meditation:

> When I reflect on myself, I not only know that I am
> something incomplete, and dependent on another, which
> incessantly aspires after something which is better
> and greater than myself, but I also know that He on
> whom I depend possesses in Himself all the great things
> toward which I aspire (and the ideas of which I find

within myself), and that not indefinitely or potentially alone, but really, actually, and infinitely, and that thus He is God.

Within this paragraph is contained the basic formula for loving God. If we believe that we are made in God's image, and yet recognize that we are unable to equal the model, we can then love that which we aspire to, namely, the fulfillment of our potentialities and the perfecting of our natures. Since we can always see a condition better than the one we are in—for no matter how excellent we are at something, we can always conceive of being better at it— we always have something to desire. This desire is mingled with a love for the desired state or object, and love becomes a continuous striving upward. Because man is finite and can never reach perfection, can never be like God, he will always be able to love God. And as the force of gravity is stronger the closer an object is to the center of the force, so will a man's love for God increase as he grows older and wiser. And thus a man who has studied and contemplated all his life, and devoted himself to improving himself and imitating God, will love God more strongly and earnestly than a youth who has just begun to look upward.

There have always been two types of humanists. There is the theological humanist, the one who believes strongly in God and in his goodness; this type of humanist rejoices in showing the similarity between God and man. He dwells on the constancy of reason and the laws of logic, and argues that since both man and God share in the quality of reason, and since this is the primary distinction between man and God and the rest of existence, man and God share the same essential nature. In fact, these humanists argue, man differs from God mostly in terms of his mortality, a mortality which keeps him from knowing all and from achieving absolute goodness.

The other type of humanist does not dwell on the similarity of man and God, but concentrates instead on the differences between man and the nonhuman animal. Man, says this humanist, does not walk on four legs with his head always facing the ground; rather, man walks on two feet with his back straight and his eyes pointing toward the heavens, so that he can study nature and gaze beyond the fuzzy atmosphere of earthly considerations. What distinguishes man from the animal is his reason, and if he acted as he ought, man would be full of every nobility.

Both types of humanists look upon man as a noble creature, and whether one takes "love of God" as representing that which we have in common with God, or that by which we differ from the animals, a striving after this love is represented by mankind as a kind of self-love, but of one's self not as it is, but as it ought to be.

If we are successful in comprehending this abstract standard of values, we are able to love God, the idea of God, and the idea of the absolute. If we believe that we can in some way commune with God, we are then able to pray, and to pray for self-improvement. We might consider, for example, and try to make our own the prayer of Francis of Assisi:

O Lord, make me the instrument of thy peace,
Where there is hatred, let me sow love,
Where there is injury, pardon,
Where there is darkness, light,
Where there is sadness, joy,
Where there is doubt, faith,
And where there is despair, hope.

O divine Master, grant that I may not so much seek
To be consoled as to console,
To be understood as to understand,
To be loved as to love.

For
It is in giving that we receive,
It is in forgiving that we are pardoned,
And it is in dying that we are born to eternal life.

It has long been understood that the Old Testament says, "The beginning of wisdom is fear of the Lord." Is fear of God compatible with love of God? In earlier chapters we have seen that the greatest obstacle to love is fear. Should it be different in this case? Or is wisdom to be rejected in favor of love? Certainly many have looked with suspicion on those who sought wisdom as though wisdom somehow reduced one's capacity for love. Does it?

In order to unravel this knotty problem, we must first examine the meaning of the statement, "Fear of the Lord is the beginning of wisdom," and we must examine the nature of this "fear." The word in Hebrew is *yirah*, and it properly refers to the trepidation, awe, reverence which one should have before and toward God. *Fear*, as we generally employ the term, is far too strong to represent precisely what *yirah* means. When, for example, one must meet an important person, a president, a famous writer, a great scientist, one has a sense of trembling and awe. One sees in the great individual talent, power, knowledge— qualities one lacks to the same degree—and one feels his smallness in comparison. The primary feeling, though, is one of awe. Such is the feeling we are expected to have toward God, and such is what the Bible means. Plato, who represents a tradition wholly different from the Hebrew, writing in the *Theaetetus*, says similarly that "philosophy begins in wonder," a statement that became an aphorism in antiquity. It is wonder which is the beginning of wisdom and philosophy, and not fear.

But what is fear of God? Fear of God may be the fear of being punished. God, in the view of those who fear Him, is a father, ready to punish any transgressions, any be-

havior which differs from his commandments. This type of
fear has been promulgated by many religions and religious
societies in order to promote morality among the citizens.
In times when an intensely personal God has been worshipped, this type of fear has prevailed. In antiquity, for
example, when the idea of a personal god was so extensive
that each person believed his own household had special
gods, fear and superstition were widespread. The Roman
philosopher Lucretius wrote his poem *The Nature of
Things* in large part to disprove the idea of personal gods.
Fear of God in this sense may be harmful to the individual,
especially when it creates excessive anxiety about violating God's commandments.

Fear of the concept of God, as we have expressed it in
this chapter, means fear of looking at the spiritual world of
love and justice that God represents. It means fear of any
absolute standard or idea. So long as one believes that
everything is relative, he may do just as he pleases, feeling that morality ought to be left wholly up to the individual, that nothing is good or bad except what appears so
to one's mind. The human being fears that if there is an
absolute, when he is measured against it he will appear as
nothing, a worm crawling in the mud.

Fear of God often comes about when man wrongly
deduces that the idea of God leads to a degrading view of
man. If, though, we see ourselves as made in God's image
and as participants in creation, man is not in the slightest
downgraded by a concept of God.

Religion, including love of God, has been called by Marx
the opiate of the people and by Freud a social obsessive-
compulsive neurosis. However, there is no doubt that most
men have a natural inclination to experience the transcendental or to aspire to it. When society compels or per-
suades them to give up this tendency, they may embrace a
political ideology that acts as a stronger kind of opiate, or
they may really develop an individual obsessive-compul-

sive syndrome, as Frankl has described. They may also succumb to cheap forms of mysticism such as astrology. Our century, no matter how intensely permeated by the impact of science and technology, has retained a longing for a spiritual reality.

Though there may be some communion between man and God, man should not become proud or arrogant. The Talmud says, "Every man who is filled with an arrogant spirit is as though he had worshipped idols." In other words, such a man does not preserve the distinction between the primitive pagan mentality and one more civilized. He worships himself instead of a separate absolute deity. Man should realize that his place is on earth and remember that the word *human* derives from the Latin *humus*, which means "earth."

In our opinion, love of God includes love for immanence —that is, for what is already here visibly created by God— and for transcendence—or for what is beyond the limit of our experience. Love for the transcendental is experienced as a belief in, and movement toward, a spiritual world which is intertwined with the material world and yet to some extent remains beyond it. The individual who is enriched by such love feels a pull for what is boundless, eternal, infinite, and inexpressible. This spirituality is experienced not just as an unknown, but as a source of a spiritual growth which reveals itself as authentic, impossible to prove objectively, yet impossible to reject subjectively. People who do not experience this movement or pull remain restrained by the limits of immanence, and eventually, if they continue their reductionistic course, by mere facts. They become factual. What man can do with this approach to transcendence will be discussed further in Chapter 12.

According to Fromm, love for God is, from a psychological point of view, not different from the other loves: "it springs from the need to overcome separateness and to achieve union." We may add that it is a special way of overcoming separateness. It is not what used to be called *unio mystica*, which was believed to consist of total absorption of the individual into God. Aloneness is not remedied by union with a personal God, but by loving God through what He has created in this immanent world and through our efforts to go beyond immanence. Love for God thus includes everything and can make any demands.

The words of St. Paul, "Love bears all things, believes all things, hopes all things, endures all things," found a concrete enactment in Abraham's willingness to sacrifice Isaac, as described in Genesis. How is this biblical story to be interpreted? Abraham received an order from God to go to Mount Moria to sacrifice his son Isaac. How could God ask so much? Should Abraham disregard God's call, or should he obey God and commit a crime against his own son? Kierkegaard interpreted Abraham's willingness to obey God as a "teleological suspension of the ethical." Ethically speaking, says Kierkegaard, a father should love his son more dearly than himself. Abraham acted in violation with this ethic. Whereas the tragic hero remains within the ethical, Abraham "overstepped the ethical and pursued a higher end."

Were we to follow usual human feelings, we would feel not only that Abraham was willing to act unethically and perpetrate murder, but would act against the dictates of family love, for Isaac was his son; against love for the other, for Isaac was a fellow human being; against self-love, for Isaac was his only son and was the most meaningful part of Abraham's life; and against love for work and ideals, for Abraham had concentrated in Isaac most of his care and concern. Isaac was expected to be the progenitor of a great people, chosen to transmit to the world Abraham's revelation of the One God, the God of Love who cannot be seen but is everywhere.

Thus love for Isaac did not mean only love for Isaac,

but for everything which was meaningful to Abraham, including love for humanity, which through Isaac would be blessed by the knowledge of God. In other words, love for Isaac came to be almost the equivalent of love for whatever God makes us love, that is, of love for God. By making such a request to Abraham, who was the first to discover love for God, God compelled Abraham to see the dimensions of such love. Once Abraham understood the magnitude of this love for God, God stopped him. "Abraham, Abraham. . . . Lay not thine hand upon the lad, neither do thou any thing unto him. . . ." Thus what started as a sacrifice of Isaac ended by being only a "binding of Isaac." The "binding of Isaac," by which name the story has been called in the Hebrew tradition, may mean not only that Isaac was bound as part of the sacrificial procedure, but was also bound to the greatest possible love, love of God. If Kierkegaard is correct in calling Abraham's attitude a suspension of ethics, we must add that this suspension did not imply readiness to violate ethics. In his infinite love of God, Abraham had faith that God would find an ethical solution. What is called suspension of ethics was required to demonstrate the extent of that love for God which for the first time in the history of the universe had entered into a human heart.

PART TWO

LOVE BETWEEN
MAN AND WOMAN

7: EROTIC
OR ROMANTIC LOVE

All types of love are sources of inspiration, concern, and growth, but the love between man and woman has stirred the deepest feelings and the broadest imaginations. Dante experienced his love for Beatrice as a journey transcending whatever is human and terrestrial and leading to salvation and encounter with the Divine. A passionate love for the beautiful Helen caused the Trojan War, the conflict which has astonished Western minds for more than 2,500 years because of its ferocity and primacy in time and because it inspired Homer's *Iliad*, the noblest epic of the West. The second epic of the West, Homer's *Odyssey*, celebrates the marital fidelity and love between Penelope and Odysseus. The encounter of Aeneas and Dido in Virgil's epic the *Aeneid* reveals the folly that springs from uncontrolled erotic desire.

Love between man and woman, often called erotic or romantic love, generally does not come into being until the partners have attained a certain level of maturity, that is, until their human qualities are fairly well developed, not before the age of puberty and at times a good deal later. This romantic love brings the strongest degree of that tendency to approach, which we have described at the beginning of this book. In fact, the tendency that the two lovers have to approach each other is so strong as to become almost a tendency to a fusion of the two, in a state of tenderness and intimacy. The fusion seems realized in the sexual act, when it appears almost as if the two bodies have become one flesh and the private feeling of one partner is not felt, like any other feeling, by one person, but by two, in a shared or fused experience.

Let us clarify from the beginning, however, that the tendency to fusion is not going to be realized, and this is most fortunate. The two partners, who love each other intensely, want to form a unity, a couple, but not a fusion. The concept of fusion is a fantasy shared by many people and idealized by some poets and artists who perhaps reactivated the old fantasy that, according to some writers, the baby entertains. It is questionable whether the baby wants to be fused with mother or perceives no boundaries between himself and the mother. He wants to be very close to mother and enjoy her tenderness, the softness of her embrace, and the warmth of her body, but he wants to be *he*, so that he can enjoy her. One could think of the baby as being fused with the mother when he was a fetus, but not after he was born. Any tendency to affectionate approach leads not to fusion but to the formation of a *bond of love*.

Erotic love constitutes a strong bond which is related to all the other bonds of love that we have so far described. When a man loves a woman, or vice versa, the loved person tends to become a member of the family or as much as is possible without genetic bonds. Also the beloved comes to represent *the other* in one's life, and becomes the repository for a gamut of neighborly and friendly feelings. In loving a member of the other sex, we are loving ourselves in the highest sense of loving what we would like to become; for what we love in the other person are those qualities which we ourselves lack, and by loving them in the other, by possessing them in the other, we come to complete and perfect ourselves. In addition, if there should be children born, our love for ourselves has been regenerated in them. Finally, by loving this completed ideal of human nature, we come closer to loving an absolute, whether that absolute be represented by the Divinity or by a philosophical idea.

It is important, certainly, to remember the differences as well as the similarities between the different objects of love. For example, we would not want to treat our children in the same way in which we treat our sweethearts, nor our sweethearts as we would treat our children. Again, if the love for one object becomes so intense that all others are forgotten, the situation may be worse by far than if the love were only moderate. We shall examine these possibilities in greater detail later.

For erotic love, too, as for the loves that we have previously described, a functional system is gradually built up, a complex composed of various neurophysiological and psychological levels, all acting together. Erotic love originates from biological needs, sexual desire, and the urge toward propagation. For most human beings, sexual desire is only the beginning of love, not its end; for other animal species, sexual desire is the beginning and end of erotic encounters. Animals do not know that a sexual act will lead to offspring; indeed, if sexual activity were accompanied by pain for both parties, animals would abstain and their species would become extinct. The pain that the female experiences in parturition will have no effect on sexual activity, for it is long removed from the act. For humans, sexual activity is very different, and bears the qualities of humanness that mark all other areas of human endeavor. Even if erotic love began with the biological needs of procreation, it does not end there. The functional system becomes more and more complicated and differentiated as several psychological levels, carriers of meanings and emotions, accrue over the simple biological matrix.

The difference between physical love and human romantic love has occupied the minds of thinkers and lovers from ancient times to the present. Romantic love has not always been separated from other types of love. Some philosophers have considered it simply a stage on the way to greater loves. Plato, for example, has Socrates describe a heavenly ladder of love in the beautiful dialogue, the *Symposium*. Love, says Socrates, begins with a desire for beauty. First one loves the beauty of bodies, then one sees the beauty in laws and institutions, then the beauty in sciences, until one comes to love the idea of beauty itself, separated and abstracted from all other considerations. For Descartes, the object of love does not matter, whether it be a person, an animal, or a habit, for the feeling toward the object is one of kindness and good will, and thus all loves have a common essential unity. Descartes distinguishes between levels of love thus: If we have less regard for the beloved object than for ourselves, we experience *affection*; if we have for it the same regard as we have for ourselves, we experience *friendship*; if we have more regard for it than for ourselves, we experience *devotion*.

Whereas most philosophers of previous epochs have stressed and welcomed the passage from sexual desire to spiritual love, there has been a reverse trend, that is, a trend to stress the sexual part of romantic love by psychoanalysts of classic Freudian orientation and by writers in other fields who have been very much influenced by Freud. We shall discuss some of these psychoanalytic points of view before we describe the various stages of romantic love and the various ways by which we can search for and obtain such a love.

PSYCHOANALYTIC CONCEPTIONS OF LOVE

It is indeed difficult to discuss psychoanalytic conceptions of love because, unbelievable as it may seem, this is a topic very much neglected by psychoanalysis. In the index of most psychoanalytic (but we could also add psychological and psychiatric) books, the word *love* is not even listed. In its place we generally find such terms as *libido* and *sex*.

Freud considers love to be a derivation of the libido or sexual instinct. This libido, which manifests itself very early in life, aims at the reproduction of the species and causes the pleasant, voluptuous sensations felt in the so-called erotogenic areas of the body. During what Freud calls a "latency period," from four years of age to puberty, the instinct lies quiescent and subdued, not to reemerge fully until the time of puberty. According to Freud, the advent of a spiritual romantic love, of a moral sense, and, indeed, the development of civilization result from inhibiting and sublimating our sexual impulses. Love is libido that was inhibited, could not therefore reach its natural biological aim, and was diverted or sublimated toward other pursuits.

Freud, unlike Plato or Descartes, who both saw an underlying unity among the various types of love, sees a struggle between them. Spiritual, romantic, and, eventually, philosophical love are all inhibitions of sexual love. For Plato, spiritual love is a transcendence of sexual love; for Descartes, a redirection of love. Although Freud was a pioneer in recognizing the power and ramifications of sexual desire, he saw it only as a condition of tension from which the human being seeks release. Lovemaking is thus seen predominantly as a liberation from a state of tension and unrest.

The Freudian psychoanalyst Edmund Bergler sees "a precise distinction between physical sensual love and tender ideal love." He interprets this ideal love as a projection; that is, the lover sees an idealized figure in the beloved. The figure, of course, is a fantasized entity which approves and flatters the lover. The lover, thus gratified, finds a resolution of all his uncertainties and doubts.

Wilhelm Reich, to whom we shall return later, was a psychoanalyst and disciple of Freud who broke with his master early. Reich is particularly interested in sex as sex, and is concerned only secondarily with love. Accordingly, he believes that both man's social and inner lives revolve around sexuality. Reich, like the eighteenth-century philosopher Rousseau, believes that man is born good but is corrupted by society; society brutally constrains man's natural impulses, which, left alone, would lead to a free, joyful, and happy sexual life. The individual, as a result, becomes self-effacing and neurotic. If one's sexual desires are frustrated in adolescence, one may become a juvenile delinquent or a sexual deviant.

In Freud's theoretical framework, the sexual instinct and the death instinct belong to the id, that primitive part of the mind which is a "seething cauldron of energy." It is an arduous task on the part of the other two divisions of the psyche, the ego and the superego, to control the id. For Reich, the id should not be so controlled, for the id is authenticity, beauty, pleasure, freedom.

Reich asks why life is not free and sexuality uninhibited. His answer is that a patriarchal society like ours imposes restrictions. First it forbids sexuality in children; they are not allowed to masturbate or to engage in sexual play with their contemporaries. Later, society tries to restrict sexuality as thoroughly as possible. The result is that the individual builds up a character armor which inhibits him sexually, diminishes his freedom, and compels him to obey society's economic and political rules. The inhibition of sexual impulses makes the human being docile and willing to submit to the authorities of the Establishment. Reich strongly believed that either through therapy or through changing society we must destroy this character structure which imprisons man.

Reich believes that even Freud, the man who discovered how greatly sexuality is repressed, succumbed to the political, economic, and social influences of his time and thus continued the practice of repression. Because of his error, Freud continued to think that the ego should control the id. According to Reich, the Freudian concept that culture and civilization are made possible by renouncing or sublimating instinctual desires is utter nonsense. The supposed connection between sexual deprivation and cultural development exists only in a capitalistic society where work is organized to satisfy the wishes of only that minority which owns the means of production.

Influenced by the writings of Bachofen and others, Reich argues that a matriarchal society would be permissive toward sexuality. There would be no artificial divisions, political or sociological. Man would grow free, unencumbered by any character armor.

Herbert Marcuse, although primarily a sociologist and political theoretician, deals extensively with the sexuality of love. Marcuse believes that Freud's greatest merit consists of having emphasized the biological-sexual components of the psyche. At a time (the 1950s) when the emerging American neo-Freudian schools of psychoanalysis were challenging the tenets of Freud, especially his theories of sex and libido, Marcuse reaffirmed the importance of sexuality in understanding the psyche. Like Reich, Marcuse feels that Freud, while deserving credit for discovering the role of sexuality in human affairs, did not do enough to liberate it from the cultural forces which repress it. According to Marcuse, society has remained far too oppressive.

Marcuse gives a political and sociological explanation for this repression. Sexuality is first focused on the genital organs while the rest of the body is gradually deprived of sexual feelings. When this desexualization is accomplished, says Marcuse, the body is used only for work; it becomes an instrument of labor. Marcuse argues that the whole body ought to be made again an instrument of sexual pleasure. According to him, the human being desires a state of "polymorphous perversity," and what are called aberrations may be partially interpreted as protests against reducing sex to the genital organs. Marcuse believes that if people had been allowed to indulge more in sexuality, they would have been less efficient as instruments of labor. Here, according to him, lies the origin of the Establishment's antagonism toward sexuality. Marcuse has also revised the anthropological hypothesis expressed by Freud in *Totem and Taboo*. The sons who, according to Freud, in prehistoric times killed their father, were not merely the sexual rivals of their father; they were proletarians exploited by a capitalist father who wanted from his children too little sex and too much work. According to Marcuse, it is not the family but society which is antagonistic to sex. But now that modern industry permits a reduction of the working day, now that the necessities of life can be available to all citizens, there is more time and energy available for sexual pleasure.

It is true that sexuality has been repressed by civilization. We must remember, however, that some repression was necessary for the safety of any organized social group. Even in primitive tribes, marital laws that restrict sexual activity have the effect of limiting rivalries and of clarifying parentage and the inheritance of property, and thus contribute to the security and stability of the nascent society.

But excessive fear and suppression of sexuality has damaged healthy psychological relations. The Victorian Era was the culmination in the excessive repression of sexuality. In criticizing Freud, Reich seems correct in denying so vigorously the connections between an individual's sexual suppression and the development of civilization. Even if we know of persons who have not accomplished anything culturally worthwhile because they concentrated all their efforts on sexual exploits, we know also of people who enjoyed a very rich sexual life and yet contributed greatly to civilization. Marcuse may be right in asserting that there has been too much sexual repression. Other of his concepts, however, are questionable. It is not true, at least for the majority of people, that sexuality has been removed from the rest of the body and confined to the sexual organs. In the human being, more than in any other animal, sex involves the whole body, although on account of physiological circumstances, the genitals remain the culminating organs in the sexual encounter. The kiss, the caress, the embrace, the touch, retain and claim their place in the act of love.

It is also not true that the body has been desexualized for the purpose of making it an instrument of labor. The restrictions on sexuality have different functions; as we just said, strict marital and sexual laws prevented rivalry and bloodshed in primitive societies. The prohibition against incest served to reduce intrafamilial and intratribal strife. In those times, all members of the same group needed to cooperate and work together against common dangers, such as enemies or famine.

In contrast to other animal species, sexual desire is almost constant in young human beings, and it seeks prompt satisfaction unless restrictions are imposed. But immediate satisfaction leads to rivalry for the favor of the best sexual partners and to revenge in cases of frustration. Primitive societies presumably had to devise and enforce strong rules to prevent hostilities. As Freud described in *Totem and Taboo*, the inhibition of sexuality which civilization requires probably originated as a device to curb the violence which sexual desires once caused. We still generally abide by the laws of marriage and incest which were instituted in primitive times.

If we can draw some general conclusions about the works of Freud, Reich, and Marcuse, we immediately recognize the important contributions they have made to the study of eroticism. Yet all of them have been unable to go deeply into the realm of love. For Freud, sexual desire must be inhibited so that man can reach his level of love and civilization. Although Reich and Marcuse have added to Freud's conceptions and have shown how sex is also connected with the political and economic organization of society, they stress sex as sex, not as an activity which may lead to higher human possibilities. Reading Reich and Marcuse, one would be led to believe that once an era of sexual permissiveness is established, the world will be a place of joy and happiness. Well, the era of sexual permissiveness is already here. There have been few times in Western history when the consummation of sex was so easy. The invention of the contraceptive pill and the legalization of abortion have enormously facilitated sexual practices. Yet we are far from a state of bliss. Psychological malaise and discontent, alienation, and insecurity have not decreased, but increased. We do not want, of course, to advocate a return to Victorian sexual suppression, but wish to stress that it is simplistic to believe that total sexual gratification will bring about happiness for all and the end of every neurosis. *It is much more appropriate to recognize a major cause of the malaise of our times not in scarcity of* sex, but in scarcity of love of all kinds, including that between men and women.

When we arrive at the neo-Freudian school of psychoanalysis we enter a different environment and begin to hear of the connections between sex and love. Erich Fromm has made some important contributions to the understanding of all types of love. According to him, the human being becomes aware of his separateness from nature. This awareness causes him great anxiety, which he tries to conquer with love. Through love he achieves union and overcomes the human being's separateness from nature. Erotic love is a craving for union, but it must be a union that preserves one's own individuality and integrity. Fromm strongly criticizes Freud for considering love a sublimation of sex and for not recognizing "that the sexual desire is one manifestation of the need for love and union."

Rollo May stresses two major components of love: eros and the daimonic. In May's theoretical framework, eros is not sex but a conflict with sex. Whereas eros is what attracts us, "draws us from ahead, sex pushes us from behind." Whereas sex is lust, eros is the drive of love to procreate and to create—the urge toward higher forms of being and relationship. Sex is not derived from but incorporated and transcended in eros. Eros is the source of tenderness, the longing to establish the full relationship which leads to union. The daimonic is a natural function which has the power to take over the whole person. Sex and eros may become daimonic, or, when constructive, may lead to dialogue and integration, or, when destructive, to decay and isolation. With Fromm and May, we breathe a different air. The biological qualities of love between man and woman are not what is emphasized; the stress is rather toward higher aims.

If a criticism of Fromm and May has to be made, it is

perhaps that they have gone too far in the other direction, and have not given enough importance to sex. We must surely go far beyond sex in any study of romantic love. But sex is one of the basic parts of this love and has to be considered, too. We shall do so in Chapter 8. In the rest of this chapter we shall describe how romantic love is experienced and how it is pursued. We shall divide this experience into three stages: (1) the stage of longing; (2) the initial stage; and, finally, (3) love as a steady flow.

ROMANTIC LOVE AS A PSYCHOLOGICAL EXPERIENCE

Longing for love at first seems to be not love itself but an antecedent of love. And yet it may be included in the psychological phenomenon of love because unless this longing develops in manifest or latent forms, no romantic love will follow. At a certain age a person experiences a desire for a state of intense relatedness, generally with a person of the opposite sex. At times this longing manifests itself predominantly as a strong sexual desire directed toward one specific person. At other times it manifests itself predominantly as a craving for tender mutuality, which consists of affectionate companionship, reciprocal concern and care, and sharing of meaningful experiences, actions, and aims. In all these cases the individual who experiences the longing feels that relief and joy would come from approach or closeness to the loved object.

This longing can exist at any age after puberty, but unless satisfied, it becomes particularly intense in the twenties. At this age there is also a passionate desire to break the state of aloneness, loneliness, and privacy that any human being, by being a separate center of consciousness, experiences. One is willing to lose this state of privacy only in regard to the person one loves. By no means do we imply that a lover should have no privacy whatsoever from the person he loves, but certainly the bond of love which implies so much communality and sharing reduces that privacy.

A person who has no romantic love never stops longing for it. If such longing does not exist, we are bound to believe that there is something wrong with him or her, at least until we know of a good reason for so great a renunciation.

A person who longs for love is in a state of restlessness and experiences a sense of emptiness which is difficult to tolerate.

Although this longing may have been perpetuated by evolution as a device to propagate the human species, it has become an important method of growth by providing the experience of intimate living with another adult and the experience of parenthood. One's personal identity becomes eventually stabilized by the enduring love that follows the longing period.

Longing for love is experienced by both men and women. Nevertheless, because our society is predominantly patriarchal and has not yet achieved a state of equality of sexes, longing for love, statistically speaking, is experienced more intensely by women. Whereas many young men give priority to the pursuit of a career, many women are most of all concerned with searching for love.

We mentioned before that we must think of the possibility of a psychological abnormality in a person who has not yet found romantic love and does not seem to miss it. We must also be aware, however, of the opposite situation. There are some people, more frequently women, who seem to have only one purpose in life: the search for love. A life without romantic love does not seem worthwhile to them. Consequently they consume all their energies in such a search, and at times they accept all compromises, all types of settlements for the sake of being loved. What results is a neglect of all the other areas of life with consequent impoverishment of the personality and decrease in the power to elicit love in others. Generally when this search for love is out of proportion or becomes so obsessive and oppressive as to prevent the pursuit of other aims, the individual has various psychological problems, for instance, the fear of being unlovable, the wish to be reassured that he (she) is acceptable, that he (she) will not be rejected and alone for a lifetime. Extreme states of dependency and dread of abandonment are at the basis of this intense longing—problems that in most instances stem from childhood, from a fear (justified or fantasied) of not being loved and taken care of by mother and/or father.

The initial stage of love is what some people call falling in love. "Falling in love" is not a good designation. It seems to imply that prior to being in love the person in question was in a superior or upright position. Falling in love seems a happening to avoid, like any type of fall. It reminds us of the French *tomber malade*. Actually, in loving there is an elevation of the human spirit. When a person begins to acknowledge to himself that he has found the appropriate partner, he feels happy, joyful, and lucky. He experiences a renewal of vigor, initiative, hope, and faith. Finally he relates to another human being with an easiness and pleasure which seem to have a magical, exclusive quality. It seems to him a magical event that the partner was born, is there near him, and is exactly as she is.

The term "falling in love" fits the conceptions of those authors (Balint, Christie) who see predominantly infantile elements in such a state: a mutual regression which is a combination of our animal inheritance, psychological immaturity, and patterns of child rearing. We believe instead that in normal persons the initial stage of love is represented more by positive than by negative or regressive qualities. Even the overevaluation of the loved person is part of the human desire to rise above facts, to go beyond, to improve. We shall return to this subject in chapters 12 and 14.

Christie follows other authors in believing that "much of the behavior of two people in love can best be understood ... in terms of regression to a blissful and mutual parent-infant (usually mother-infant) style of tenderness and caring, with each person taking turns in playing the role of mother or infant. The use of name diminutives and even baby talk by young lovers is very common, of course. And many ballads, love poems, and popular songs contain mother-infant imagery ..." We wish to stress that even if the relation appears regressive, it is inherently not at all like that of a parent and an infant. Its distinctive characteristic is that the lovers are in a relationship of partnership or equality. No parent is there to scold a child or play with him. The climate of love which is generated includes not only intense involvement and commitment, but also permissiveness and at times even a shared return to some blissful times of early childhood.

The initial stage of love may become a "fall" or an abnormal infatuation when it is characterized by an all-engrossing preoccupation, by inability to wait, by incessant fear that the love will not last and therefore has to be made irrevocable at once. A disproportionate demanding attitude, an anxiety about the possibility of even a short separation, and an intolerance for even the smallest frustration are also characteristics of the abnormal infatuation. If the partner does not telephone exactly at the expected time, he seems to send the ominous and dreaded signal that the relation is going to end.

The third and most important stage of romantic love is the one which follows the initial and which in normal and desirable circumstances is best designated as a *steady flow*. With this term we mean an enduring type of love, not easily shaken or threatened by daily events or by unusual happenings, a relation founded on mutual attraction, trust, and faith. This state of reliance does not indicate that this type of love is a perpetual and unperishable good, to be kept in reserve for continuous use once it has been obtained, but something that will continue its steady flow if cherished and cultivated. As a matter of fact, love, although probably immutable in its basic core, does change and acquire new meanings at different ages. The steady flow of love is a form of relatedness and exchange transmitted through bodies which touch, embrace, kiss, and unite, through messages of endearment and approval, through words which exchange feelings, ideas, and promote joy and balms to wounds. The state of being together gives a new dimension to everything. What love makes intense at a certain age, it makes more serene and tender at a later period of life.

Although it is possible to be in love with a person who does not respond or who is forced to be absent or is dead, in these cases the situation is under stress and can be maintained only with a determination equal in strengh to the nature of the devotion and commitment.

THE SEARCH FOR LOVE

If romantic love is so desirable and wanted by everybody, why does it seem so difficult to find? Let us first of all dismiss a doubt. Most men and women do find love in their lives. It is a fact, however, that a considerable minority of people have trouble in finding love or in maintaining a loving relation, and a large number of them seek psychotherapeutic help for this reason. Numerically speaking, in searching for this help they are second only to those who have definite psychiatric disturbances. Unusual, specific circumstances make it difficult to find romantic love in some cases. If we exclude, however, people who are severely handicapped by physical or psychiatric conditions, we can say that most people can pursue romantic love successfully. The following ten recommendations can help a large number of people.

1. Overcoming personal fears

The first and most important recommendation involves the specific fear of not finding a person to love, the fear of being always rejected, and the fear of being committed. The conquest of fear requires courage and understanding, as we have discussed in Chapter 1. Most of the fears are based on those conditions described earlier in this book, which also interfered with the development of family love, love for the other, and self-love. We have thus another indication that these loves are the best prerequisites for a successful pursuit of romantic love.

A person must seek romantic love even if he is afraid, but he will be in a better position to achieve his goal if he has discovered the existence of all the fears that we have described, has traced back their causes and neutralized their effects. A fearful, hesitant, trembling person is likely not to show his best qualities and has less chance of eliciting a positive reaction in a potential partner.

2. Belief in self-worth and dignity

This second recommendation is actualized almost automatically after the fears have been conquered. Any person who is no longer at the mercy of the frightening forces that used to subjugate him becomes aware of his human dignity, has self-respect, considers himself worthy of love, and thinks that it is his inalienable right to search for love.

In order to have such a right it is not necessary to be endowed with exceptional beauty, intelligence, or wealth. What is necessary is the belief that every human being with a loving attitude has the possibility of finding a partner suitable to his or her condition. Although it is true that in many respects each person is unique, no one is so dissimilar from others or so unusual in his set of qualities as to be incompatible with every other member of the human race.

A person who has faith in himself radiates security, affects favorably surrounding persons, and promotes a loving attitude. It goes without saying that belief in self-worth promotes self-assertion, but not grandiosity, pomposity, or self-inflation. It is part of one's belief in self-worth and self-dignity to acknowledge one's limitations with graciousness and humility.

3. Exposure

The person who seeks romantic love must expose himself to situations in which he is likely to meet a partner, that is, to situations where people of approximately the same age and interests are apt to be present.

Quite often we hear people say that they do not want to force destiny. If things are supposed to happen, they will happen. People who think in this way secretly long for love and secretly continue to entertain fantasies conceived in childhood or early adolescence—variations of the fantasy that one day a knight will appear on a white horse, will knock at the door, and will bring the engagement ring to the girl who was waiting for him. These fantasies, which, with the proper variation, occur in both sexes, indicate a frame of mind of passivity. They actually reveal that fear still exists in the person who entertains such fantasies, as well as doubt about being worthy of actively seeking love. These fantasies, as experienced espe-

cially by women, have been the object of much consideration and are a recurring theme, both in great literature as
well as in popular stories, fairy tales, jokes, and so forth.
Tennessee Williams' poetic and touching play *The Glass
Menagerie* portrays a young woman who expects a "gen-
tleman caller" to ring the bell, to love her at first sight, and
to marry her. But such a passive role, sustained only by
wishful thinking, does not lead to the wanted outcome. In
this beautiful play, the first of his successful ones, Williams
portrays a drama unfortunately too often repeated in many
generations of women.

Opposite is the message of the story of Cinderella, the
famous popular fairy tale which inspired many writers,
poets, and especially composers of operas, including Gio-
acchino Rossini and Jules Massenet. According to the ver-
sions given by the Frenchman Charles Perrault and the
German Wilhelm Grimm, poor Cinderella, whose mother
died when she was a child, is the victim of her stepmother,
who prefers her real daughters, and of a father who suc-
cumbs to the pressure of his tyrannical second wife. A fairy
intervenes, and makes it possible for a prince to fall in love
with Cinderella and, by finding a lost shoe, retrieve her
and marry her. Cinderella is finally compensated for all
her deprivations. The main point of the tale is that justice
is finally reestablished. Not only does Cinderella get the
love that she deserves, but she gets it from the most desirable man—a future king. Actually the story is misguid-
ing. It is true that people must deserve love, but unlike
Cinderella they must search for it and not rely on being
the instrument of a fairy of love and justice.

Similar to the Cinderella story is an Italian folk tale
founded on a popular tradition. In Italy many believe that
St. Anthony is the patron saint of girls who wish to get
married. Many single girls, desirous of love and marriage,
pray to the saint to help them, and often buy a little terra
cotta statue of the saint and address to it their prayers. The

story goes that a girl did exactly so, but, in spite of her having prayed every day to the saint, no prospective husband appeared. In a fit of indignation she grabbed the little terra cotta and threw it out the window. The statue landed on the head of a young man who happened to be walking by on the street. He turned his head up to see who had thrown it and saw the girl at the window. He immediately fell in love and soon married her. St. Anthony was vindicated once more! Tales like Cinderella and the Italian story are indicative of an archaic and infantile wish, entertained by many people, to be passive in the realm of love and to leave even vital matters to the whim of destiny. Certainly we can give a chance to chance, but we do better if we rely on our own actions. Yes, love is there to be found, but it must be actively pursued.

There are indeed many reasons that make exposure to romantic encounters difficult. In some geographical areas, like large urban centers, women generally outnumber men by far. This discrepancy is partially a result of the fact that many women leave small towns and go to the big cities to find employment. Conversely, in small towns where colleges that accept only male students are located, there is generally a greater percentage of males among faculty members and students. These difficulties are not insurmountable. Sooner or later people who are eager to find love partners will learn where encounters are likely to take place.

4. Not looking for the impossible

Some people claim that they cannot find a suitable partner. On closer examination these people reveal themselves to be searching for what is impossible or extremely difficult to find, either in any environment or in the particular place where they live. If it is very important for a person to find a love partner who belongs to the same religious or ethnic minority, he must frequent places where people of that particular minority are likely to be. Some people search for absolute honesty, authenticity, and unquestionable normality in a love partner. These requests may be legitimate, provided the terms are reasonably defined. Is being honest and authentic to be interpreted as having to stress one's shortcomings, to make sure that the would-be partner knows everything negative about one, to the tiniest detail? If one expects to be informed of every minor idiosyncrasy, it is obvious that there is a psychological need to set for oneself an impossible goal. Some young women, indoctrinated by popular psychological literature, search for a man who is not at all neurotic. But who could be certified even by a competent psychiatrist as having no neurotic traits? Obviously it is not desirable to commit oneself to a seriously neurotic person, at least until he is better, but minor neurotic traits are almost unavoidable parts of our sophisticated life, and can be accepted when they are outweighed by positive traits. Other people want to find a very mature partner. Their request seems valid, provided they have a definite and plausible concept of what maturity is. Certainly it is not advisable to settle for a partner who does not appear desirable. Candidates for romantic love must, however, take into account that in a love situation people are likely to mature together and to lose minor neuroticisms.

In some cases, however, the search for the impossible partner has more subtle, and most of the time unconscious, reasons. In these cases, a person becomes a desirable partner when he is recognized as being unavailable and therefore impossible to obtain. For instance, he is already married, is the kind of person who shows no interest in anyone who is interested in him, or is impossible to trust because he has already demonstrated himself to be deceitful and unreliable.

If a person has recurrent involvements or preoccupations

with hypothetical "impossible partners," the suspicion arises that he is acting under unconscious motivation, in connection with the Oedipal situation described by Freud. For instance, he may search for a partner similar to father or mother, who were considered impossible to get, either because already married to the other parent or because unwilling to bestow love. In these cases psychotherapy is indicated.

5. Not rushing to accept or reject

The person who seeks romantic love should not offer immediate acceptance or rejection. Love at first sight is another myth. Although it may occur, it is not the most frequent type of love, nor the most desirable. At times the traits which are conspicuous at the beginning of the acquaintance are not fundamental and may disguise others which are more important. What appears as security and strength of character may actually be callousness to feelings. What seems self-assurance may be arrogance and a covering up of extreme insecurity. What appears as timidity and hesitation may be cautiousness and wisdom. What appears as charm and gallantry may be phoniness. What appears as indecisiveness may prove to be profundity of thought and careful consideration. What seems so beautiful and convincing may be a prepared presentation, like that of a salesman, not likely to be repeated, and not likely to be followed by another which sustains equal interest.

6. Asking yourself why you are often rejected

If a young person realizes that he is often rejected by a person who at first seemed genuinely interested, he must ask himself why the change occurred. Does he fear warmth, and therefore follow an unconscious pattern of behavior that makes him appear undesirable when closeness approaches? Is he too demanding, or too dependent, or too possessive? Is he too aggressive and seemingly interested only in a sexual encounter? Is he really looking for a mother to take care of him and not for a wife? Does she really want a father and not a husband? Does he want to be adored unconditionally? Does he want to be constantly admired, confusing admiration with love? Does he make an unwarranted identification or confusion between the woman he is considering and his mother, sister, or another woman of his past? Does she make an unwarranted identification or confusion between the man she is considering and her father, brother, or another man of her past? Does he use a sense of humor that appears offensive and undercutting? Does he take offense easily when no offense is meant? Does he make the wrong assumption that a woman must declare her love by accepting being belittled? Does he believe that to agree and to go along means to be unduly meek and submissive? Does he believe in the supremacy of the male? Does she expect too heavy a commitment, like support of the children of her former husband? Is he too inquisitive, asking very private questions when the relationship has not yet acquired a degree of closeness that makes such questions permissible? Does he make her feel inferior because she is less educated, has a less prestigious occupation, or earns less money? Does he expect from her a total commitment, although he is unable or unwilling to disentangle himself from previous ties?

The young man or woman who sees many relations come to an end after an apparently successful initial friendship must reflect on these and many more possibilities. Often a careful search will reveal the answer to the problem. The person must avoid falling into the trap of finding easy rationalizations, or of using terms that seem to explain everything but explain nothing. We shall mention just a few. One common reason given is that there was no physical attraction. Most of the time, this is not a valid reason because if there were no initial physical attraction, the relation would not have started. Quite often what seems a sudden loss of physical attraction is actually a gradually increasing dissatisfaction with the personality of the partner—dissatisfaction that is difficult to define. A second reason given is that there was incompatibility of character. This could be a good reason, of course. But again the word *incompatibility* includes vague concepts, which may be more accurately defined if one searches for the answers to the questions mentioned above.

A third reason, and one of the most unacceptable, is that "our chemistry did not go together." Here the lack of clarity is enormous. The explanation seems to include either the body or the psyche. It is vague in every way.

7. Sustaining the longing

This recommendation is difficult for many young people to understand. If an initial relationship seems a promising one, the two involved persons should not seek immediate and total gratification in terms of availability in companionship, sex, intellectual exchange, and so on. A promising love is made to grow not only by what goes on *between* the two partners when they are together, but also by what goes on *inside* each of them when they are not together. In the initial stage love receives nourishment not just by mutual exchange, but by thinking, daydreaming, fantasying, and missing the absent. That longing for love which preceded the encounter must be followed now by a longing for the specific person one is involved with. As we shall see again in Chapter 14, what makes love grow consists not only of elements of reality, no matter how pleasant they are, but of what transcends the experiences. It consists of symbols that the partners consciously or unconsciously give to the experiences and by so doing enrich and expand them. These symbols are often expressed in poetic terms. They refer both to the experience of love and to the sustained longing. When the darkness of the night surrounds your lover with silence and aloneness, let him think of you and he will not be lonely. When he rejoices for whatever reason, let him think and wish you were there to share the joy. When his soul hurts, let him think that if you were there, you would console him. When he thinks of you and you are not there, he may think you think he thinks of you—almost as if you could hear him. Whenever he sees beauty and grace, he will see your features, but if he does not, he wishes you to be there and see beauty with him. Remember that if too much contact and gratification occur in the beginning, facts and experiences will prevail to such an extent as not to allow the symbolism of love to develop; your love will be like a seed which soon after it is sown receives too much water and will not grow to be a mature plant.

The opposite situation, which is of much less frequent occurrence today, also deserves consideration. If one of the partners makes himself hardly available after a prolonged relationship, the other partner may feel frustrated and become disenchanted. Longing must be sustained at the proper, initial time, but not unnecessarily prolonged.

8. No misrepresentation

If at the beginning of the relationship one misrepresents himself, he is heading for trouble. The truth about one's age, health, religion, general philosophy of life, major past events, major interests, long-range prospects, hopes, and aspirations must be stated. Your partner in love must trust you. The discovery of a major misrepresentation will be a fatal blow to the incipient relationship.

9. Not expecting success with every trial

There are some people who become discouraged when a blind date, a meeting, an encounter, does not lead to the establishment of an enduring relationship. This is indeed too much to expect. To expect to be accepted as a love partner whenever one meets an eligible person means either to have a grandiose, pompous vision of oneself, or to expect the other person to exert no selection whatsoever, to accept everybody indiscriminately. This would mean either thinking that the other person's judgment is poor or expecting that he confuses romantic love with neighborly love. Nobody, in relation to a special role, is accepted by everybody. Even the President of the United States, when he is elected, can be rejected by 49 percent of the voters. In romantic love the percentage needs to be much, much smaller. We need only *one* partner.

10. Commitment

The final recommendation is the one that we have made throughout this book, and therefore one that does not need to be stressed again. In the search for love we cannot be amateurish or halfhearted. No dilettantism, but seriousness and perseverance are required.

MAINTAINING THE STEADY FLOW

Once love has been found, it has to be preserved; it does not continue automatically in its steady flow. Again we must stress that we cannot confuse serenity, reliance, loyalty, and trust with passivity, taking things for granted, and living on past laurels.

The closeness that the steady flow of love requires may bring forth to the utmost the beauties of the physical and personal intimacy, but also difficulties, which may occur when they are least expected. The beauties and the difficulties may involve specifically the sexual area or the total romantic union, as we shall see in the following chapters.

8: THE SEXUAL DIMENSION

SEX AND LOVE

For the first time in evolution, radical changes occur in the human anatomy. The head is freed from mechanical movements. The skull is able to expand; the brain enlarges. The human animal stands erect; two limbs change from feet to hands, and with hands the human being becomes a maker, as well as a person who can embrace another. The mouth is no longer used as a seeker of food, but as a consumer of what has been found by other organs and as one of the main parts of the instrument of language.

With the upright posture the male and female for the first time look at one another during the sexual encounter. The lips of the partners protrude so that they touch one another in a kiss; the eyes mirror the image of the beloved;

the soft round breasts of the female press against the chest of the male. While the partners consummate the sexual act, they embrace one another; and unless they prefer to avoid such result, they can foresee the possible propagation of an offspring who will constitute a blending of their two selves.

Even anatomically, the human sexual act permits a total and intimate closeness; it is not limited to the genital organs unless the partners so limit it. Whereas most animals experience the sexual urge only during mating periods, sexual desire in the human after puberty is almost constant; moreover, it is generalized in the whole body, and reaches, especially in the female, a prolonged and intensified culmination. When encountering another human being in the sexual act, it is difficult not to have strong feelings of affection toward the partner, not to talk, kiss, hug. It is, of course, possible to reduce the encounter to a genital union; this is often done by people who seek sexual release by means of prostitution. Some people resort to prostitution when no better opportunity exists to relate to the other sex. The principal cause for this lack of opportunity is fear of a total encounter, already discussed in the previous chapter.

Even when a sexual encounter is entirely satisfactory, it constitutes only a part of erotic love. Sexual pleasure may be the precursor of another type of pleasure that consists of spiritual and intangible qualities. In numerous cultures, especially those permeated by the Judeo-Christian ethic, however, the passage is expected to be not from sex to love but from love to sex. Sex is considered the physical culmination of a state of love. This sequence is possible and desirable. It is common knowledge that if two persons have already experienced spiritual affinity for each other, they will share the beauty of the sexual act in a more intense, meaningful, and diversified way.

Sex is the most sensuous color in the rainbow of love.

The direct contact of the bodies of the two partners produces an excitement which affects almost the whole organism. The nervous system, the senses, the muscles, the hormones, and the blood vessels participate intensely, but it is especially in the sexual organs that the most pronounced changes occur. All these changes begin in the foreplay, that is, in a stage of excitement which leads to the full erection of the penis in men and to vaginal lubrication in women. Lovers generally learn to prolong or to vary this stage of foreplay in order to increase the duration of the pleasant feelings. The second stage of the sexual experience is the orgasm, which is considered the apex of sexual pleasure. In the male the orgasm consists of a few spurts of semen from the penis. In the female it consists of rhythmic contractions of vaginal and perineal muscles.

As we have described it, the physiology of the sexual act seems very simple; and yet it is extremely complicated. Of course, it is out of place to deal here with the physiology of sexual functions. Let us point out immediately, however, that *to know everything you want to know about sex* is impossible, contrary to what has been claimed by some. Many readers may be surprised at such a statement. They may be more inclined to accept the idea that it is not possible to know everything about love, but why not about sex? For the simple reason that not everything is known about sex. Much has been known about sexual matters for a long time, and much has been added in the last few years (Masters and Johnson, Kaplan); but what remains to be known or understood is still an unbelievably large amount. First of all, we must stress that the sexual experience has so many variables and components that we can declare sex to be unique in each individual. Moreover, although it is true that all sexual acts have basic mechanisms in common, a great deal remains obscure even about these basic mechanisms.

SOME ASPECTS OF SEXUALITY IN WOMEN

Especially in the realm of woman's sexuality there are many unknowns. Sexuality is simpler in men. Although women experience sexual pleasure very intensely, and probably more intensely than men, we have no sure knowledge about the physiological mechanism by which this sexual pleasure is felt. Here are some of the matters that wrap woman's sexuality in mystery. We know that sexual activity is related to the endocrine glands of the body, specifically the gonads: testicles in the male, ovaries in the female. But women who have had their ovaries and uterus surgically removed maintain a normal sexual appetite and enjoy sexual intercourse with men. If, however, a man loses his testicles, he cannot achieve an erection, and almost totally loses the capacity to enjoy sexual activity. One would think that in women who had these operations late in life (because of cysts, tumors, or the like), their sexuality has developed a central organization in the nervous system. Sexual pleasure would be experienced directly by the nervous system without the intervention of hormonal intermediaries. This hypothesis is contradicted by the fact that even very young women who have hysterectomies before any sexual experience are able to enjoy sexual pleasure.

On the other hand, we do know that sexual hormones, secreted by the ovaries, have an effect on sexuality. As a matter of fact, many physicians have studied the various degrees of sexual desire during the stages of the menstrual cycle in the woman. Shortly before ovulation a small production of progesterone occurs which intensifies sexual desire. After ovulation, as progesterone production increases, the desire is heightened. Obviously, although these hormonal changes are important, they are not indispensable for sexual pleasure, which may occur even after removal of the ovaries.

How does a woman experience sexual pleasure? The woman has two organs for this purpose, the clitoris and the vagina. Many women are able to differentiate clitoral from vaginal orgasms; others are not. During the phase of excitement, the clitoris goes through a swelling reaction followed by retraction. After repeated or sustained stimulation of the clitoris, the excitement spreads to the vagina, where it finds fulfillment. But how is the sexual pleasure experienced? In the male it is relatively simple. Some sensory cells in the skin of the penis (especially in the glans) act as receptors of the stimulation, which is transmitted through the pudendal nerves and the posterial spinal roots to the spinal cord and from there to the brain. In the woman there are few genital corpuscles in the little glans of the clitoris. There are no genital corpuscles in the vagina. Pleasure must be experienced by the woman through muscular contractions. In the deeper part of the vaginal wall there are proprioceptive and stretch-sensory endings, but most women have the sensation that the pleasure extends beyond the vagina. In some women it remains limited to the pelvic organs; in others it extends to the buttocks or to the whole body. In the female it is not at all clear how the various branches of the peripheral central nervous system receive all these sensations, elaborate them in a spinal center, and then transmit them to the brain. Neurologists have ascertained that there is in the male an orgastic spinal center in the sacral portion of the spinal cord. It is assumed that a similar center exists in the female, but this has not yet been demonstrated. This center must collect sensory stimulation from a much greater area than in the male. This center, in both sexes, is connected with higher centers, probably but not definitely located in the brain stem, in the midbrain, and in what MacLean calls the limbic system.

A controversy is also still going on as to the relative importance of clitoral and vaginal responses in women. Psychoanalysts generally went along with Freud in thinking that only a vaginal orgasm is complete and fully gratifying. Recently, the psychoanalyst Natalie Shainess, although not a classical Freudian, has reaffirmed the superiority of the vaginal orgasm. But we must remember that the clitoris plays an important role in the vaginal orgasm as well. It is impossible for a woman to achieve a vaginal orgasm unless the clitoris has been stimulated first. Again, sexual stimulation starts and is sustained by the clitoris, even when the orgasm reaches a vaginal climax. Masters and Johnson believe that an orgasm involving exclusively or predominantly the clitoris should be considered satisfactory. Helen Kaplan asserts that both the clitoral and the vaginal orgasms should be accepted, conferring variety to the woman's sexual experience. According to Therese Benedek, many women who experience clitoral orgasm are unaware of the vaginal participation in this type of orgasm. Thus it seems that consensus has not been obtained, in spite of the fact that some of the most competent experts in this area are women. The prevailing point of view probably is a compromise: Although the vaginal orgasm is the richest and the most rewarding, the clitoral one should not be rejected or even minimized. It has its place, too, and is very valuable when the other cannot be achieved.

Another mystery of the vagina, or of the female sexual apparatus in general, is the fact that it does not always respond to the sexual encounter. Whereas a man who is healthy and capable of erecting can reach orgasm almost 100 percent of the time, women vary greatly in the degree and number of their responses. And whereas practically every man who does not reach orgasm feels very frustrated and unhappy, many a woman experiences a much milder degree of frustration. In fact, some women report satisfactory pleasure even when they do not reach orgasm. It seems probable, however, that cultural conditions have indoctrinated women to deny or to express less vehemently their sexual frustration. There is no doubt, though, that women who never respond to sexual encounters or who respond very rarely are very discontented, at times alienated from their husbands, and that psychological difficulties will arise.

Lack of response in women assumes different forms. Some women do not lubricate and their vaginas do not expand. Others lubricate abundantly and experience strong erotic feelings but still do not reach orgasm. In some relatively rare cases called vaginismus, the vaginal muscles contract tightly and prevent entrance of the penis. Various causes have been described for all these forms of frigidity: sociocultural, psychological in either an intrapsychic or an interpersonal sense, physiological, or some combination of them.

Those who give great weight to sociocultural causes stress that for time immemorial women have been repressed sexually much more than men, that they have been conditioned to suppress sexuality, and that now they cannot decondition themselves. In some cases, inability to respond arises from inhibitions caused by prohibition. For example, a large percentage of women who remain virgins until their wedding night are so inhibited sexually that they are not able to respond for a certain period of time. Other women feel that society compels them to be used or possessed by men. Men earn money and "buy" sex. These women cannot respond to sex, which in this socioeconomic structure of a bourgeois society, seems to them to have become an economic exchange. This attitude, facilitated by certain qualities of capitalistic society, that sex is given in exchange for economic support, alienates many women.

Oftener, however, these social causes of frigidity simply *reinforce personal causes.* Inadequate stimulation is very often a cause. The male partner is often eager to penetrate long before the female partner is ready for the sexual act. He may believe that the woman is ready. Either because he claims he cannot wait or because the reticent woman does not openly tell him that she is behind, intercourse takes place before the proper conditions are established. Inadequate stimulation is not only caused by lack of foreplay, dealing with the whole body of the female partner and especially with the clitoris, but may also be caused by premature ejaculation. If the male partner ejaculates and loses his erection, he cannot continue to stimulate the clitoris and the vaginal walls. During sex the clitoris swells and then regains its normal size. This sequence can be repeated several times during the sexual act, and provides the stimulation which is transmitted to the vagina. If the penis loses tumescence before full excitement has occurred, the woman does not reach orgasm. In these cases, of course, we cannot talk of female frigidity. If, however, the woman does not respond within ten to fifteen minutes from the time of penetration, the reason is other than her partner's premature ejaculation.

Some women cannot abandon themselves to sexual pleasure, either because they believe it unbecoming for a woman to do so or because they are afraid of being controlled and possessed by the man. If the man gives her sexual pleasure in addition to economic support, she will depend on him entirely and will become his slave, his possession. Other women force themselves not to respond because they wish to deny the man the satisfaction of their responding to his masculinity.

The orthodox school of psychoanalysis has found other reasons, buried in the unconscious, for some women's lack of participation. An unresolved Oedipus complex may contribute. According to Freud, when the woman was a little girl, she developed strong feelings for her father and strong death wishes for her rival for father's affection, her mother. She feels guilty, and feels she will be punished by being injured in her genital organs. When later she has sexual relations, she is afraid of being injured, and her original fear returns. Oftener, however, the woman unconsciously identifies her lover with her father, for whom she nourished the sexual desires that brought about the guilt feelings. The most common cause of frigidity, according to Freudian theory, is based on penis envy. When the woman was a little girl from three to five years of age, she wanted to have a penis like her brothers. She believes she has been deprived, and never comes to accept her femininity.

Most analysts and psychotherapists today believe that the relation with the father in childhood does play an important role in the development of a girl's sexuality and attitude toward men. Most, however, no longer accept the theory of penis envy. According to Clara Thompson, if the penis is envied, it is because it is a symbol of being a man, and the little girl realizes soon in life that in our patriarchal society it is more advantageous to be a man.

The Neo-Freudian schools of psychoanalysis give more importance to the entire interpersonal relationship between the woman and her husband. A sexual dysfunction is often representative of a marital situation that is not right. The sexual dysfunction, in its turn, makes the marital situation worse. A vicious circle thus perpetuates itself until it is broken.

Only in extremely rare cases is frigidity the result of arrested development of sexual glands. A woman's sexual glands may be perfect and she may still suffer from frigidity. And, on the contrary, as we said a bit earlier, a woman may have entirely lost her sexual glands and still have a normal and authentic sexual response and desire. If a woman has repeatedly been unable to respond, she may develop the fear that she will never respond. This fear may prevent her from relaxing or abandoning herself to the sexual encounter and may become an additional obstacle to her enjoyment.

Although female sexuality is still surrounded by mystery, frigidity is not an insurmountable difficulty and can be solved by removal of its causes. The social causes we have spoken of have to be eliminated, the deep conflicts uncovered, the sexual act examined without embarrassment, and the relations with the husband discussed. If the fears that sociocultural economic prejudices have instilled are overcome, if the old fear concerning the father is uncovered, if the fear of rejection or separation does not hide marital problems that could be remedied, solutions can be found. Of course, we must remember that most women do not respond 100 percent of the time. No feeling of inadequacy should be engendered if the woman should not happen to respond. The attitude of both wife and husband toward the occasional nonresponse should be examined and discussed openly and without fear.

Many women complain, "My husband does not care whether I have pleasure or not. He does not even ask me. He either takes for granted that I do or he is selfish." Other women often make an almost opposite complaint: "After we make love, my husband always asks me, 'Did you come?' That question produces in me a sick feeling. It is as though he is questioning me in order to pass me or flunk me." In view of these opposite reactions, how is a husband to act? Certainly he should not be uninterested in his wife's response. He must cooperate to the best of his ability so that she, too, can enjoy the experience. If he wants to determine whether his wife experienced pleasure or not, he must do so with delicacy and not every time they make love. He must explain to her that contrary to what some women believe, the male partner cannot always be aware of when the female partner responds. His question is not motivated by a desire to find fault in her, or in order to reject her, but in order to be a more effective partner.

SOME ASPECTS OF SEXUALITY IN MEN

Male sexuality, too, is not without an aura of mystery. The most common dysfunction is premature ejaculation; that is, the male partner has a climax, with emission of semen, either before entering the vagina or shortly afterward. How long the period of copulation should continue is a matter of debate, in spite of what we said about female response. According to Kinsey, ejaculation within one or two minutes is a normal time, since in all animal species, including monkeys and apes, very rapid ejaculation is the rule. Most experts, however, disagree with Kinsey. He does not give enough importance to the elements that enter into the *human* sexual encounter, especially the concern of the male partner for satisfying the female.

Inasmuch as women vary in the length of time they need to reach orgasm, it is often difficult to determine whether the male partner is suffering from premature ejaculation or not. There is no doubt that many men suffer from this condition. They themselves complain because their pleasure is greatly diminished, and, of course, their partners complain. Although the condition is very common and has been the object of much study, we are not sure that we know the cause of it.

The Freudian school of psychoanalysis believes that the male who ejaculates prematurely is unconsciously harboring hostile feelings toward women in general or toward a particular woman. He wants to soil her and deprive her of pleasure. There is no doubt that men can use premature ejaculation as a hostile revenge, but this happens in only a small percentage of cases; and when it happens, it is an unconscious mechanism. Even men who are genuinely in love with their wives and who want to share pleasure with them may still be unable to delay ejaculation. Masters and Johnson have advanced a "common sense" theory of premature ejaculation; bad habits acquired with prostitutes, who wanted to complete the business transaction as quickly as possible, or with girl friends in the back seats of automobiles are responsible for the condition. Their hypothesis is to be rejected in almost every case. Although it is true that prostitutes want to dispose of their clients as quickly as possible, the hurry is accomplished by omitting foreplay and by requesting that the clients undress and dress as quickly as possible. When it comes to the act of intercourse itself, prostitutes do not mind spending a few minutes more. Many people have reported that the prostitute was really sorry at the speed of ejaculation; her customer had not spent his money well, and she had not given him enough pleasure. Premature ejaculation was also very common before young people started to use the car for the sexual encounter.

The most frequent cause of premature ejaculation is anxiety or insecurity. The young man is insecure about himself in general and particularly in the sexual act, which will show whether he is a man. In a few cases the insecurity derives from a feeling of guilt, of deep origin, connected with Oedipal feelings for one's mother, as described by Freud, or with sexual activity in general, still connected with sin or illegality. Other men who suffer from premature ejaculation are afraid that they will continue to lack control and to be unable to satisfy the partner.

This anxiety in turn makes them more susceptible to premature ejaculation. Some men refer to the ejaculatory act as a reflex that they cannot control.

On the other hand, some experts (for instance, Helen Kaplan) state that ejaculation is not to be considered an involuntary reflex. The ejaculation becomes inevitable if the excitement is allowed to go beyond a certain point; but the young man must learn to control the excitement, just as earlier in his life he was able to learn to control the sphincters that regulate urination and defecation. The young man must learn the various phases of his response during the sexual act. Whenever he senses that the excitement is becoming too pronounced, he must stop all movement and cause a suspension of the response. He must learn to distinguish the different stages and control their unfolding. Although at first the procedure may require a certain effort, in the long run it will prove useful to both male and female partners. If, however, the individual is insecure or anxious, he cannot concentrate on exploring himself and arresting the stimulus.

Mechanical means of delaying the ejaculatory reflex have been devised. The urologist James Semans described a technique. While the husband has an erection, the wife stimulates his penis manually, not vaginally, until the excitement becomes very intense. Stimulation is then interrupted until the feeling disappears. The procedure is repeated. When the husband reaches the point where he can be stimulated manually without ejaculating, he will be cured of intravaginal ejaculation. Masters and Johnson have devised the so-called "squeeze" technique. When the male is about to ejaculate, the female partner places her thumb and two fingers just below the rim of the glans, thus causing a partial flaccidity. This procedure, when repeated, causes him to acquire control.

Male impotence, that is, inability to have an erection, is also a frequent disorder, although less frequent than premature ejaculation. Although in the case of impotence, too, some underlying mechanisms with a long history are at the root of the problem, fear of not performing well or of not satisfying the partner plays an important role. Some men may lose the erection if foreplay is protracted for a long time. Fear of not being able to reacquire the erection may actually become an obstacle, in a sort of circular mechanism. For more details about the conditions described above, and especially for more information about male impotence, the reader is referred to the excellent works of Helen Kaplan and Harold Lief.

SEXUAL LIFE AND LIFE

For our purposes, we must determine whether sexual difficulties may bring about marital difficulties and be an impediment to the fulfillment of love. According to Greene, sexual dissatisfaction contributes the fourth most frequent complaint in marital discord, after lack of communication, constant arguing, and unfulfilled emotional needs. In Sager's investigation, 75 percent of couples whom he saw in marital therapy had significant sexual complaints in addition to their marital problems. In our own statistics, in 60 percent of marital difficulties there are also sexual problems, but in fewer than 25 percent of the cases do sexual problems contribute the main, the fundamental, or even the most distressing symptoms. Our statistics indicate that although sexual problems may be a great handicap to the fulfillment of marital love, the inability to achieve a satisfactory love relationship more frequently has repercussions on sexual life. For instance, a relationship that is not based on equality and partnership, but in which one partner acts as either a master or a slave of the other, is bound to bring about sexual difficulties. This type of personal interaction and others will be the object of our consideration in the following chapters.

At this point it is important to stress that sexual life has symbolic manifestations that extend to the whole life of the individual. A man who happens to be impotent even on a few occasions (an occurrence much more frequent and much less serious than generally believed) may feel as if he were impotent or inadequate toward life in general. He may develop doubts about being sufficiently assertive or capable of taking any initiative. On the other hand, a woman who is afraid of being called sexually aggressive may assume an inhibitory attitude toward life in general. Sexual gratification or deprivation almost always becomes associated with such concepts as being accepted or rejected, desirable or undesirable, loved or unloved, lovable or unlovable, capable or incapable, normal or abnormal. Thus sexual behavior is allowed to affect the whole image or even the whole way of being in the world.

There is no doubt that sexual frustration makes it more difficult to build a loving, romantic relationship. On the other hand, a love that seemed firmly established may be blocked, arrested, or inhibited by ensuing sexual disorders, and is waiting for its liberation. Many people can help themselves by paying deep consideration to the issues discussed in this chapter. Often, however, professional help is necessary, and is easily available. Nevertheless, some people are afraid to search for professional help for sexual problems. Some may be embarrassed at having to reveal even to a professional person so private and intimate a matter, but a considerable number of people are afraid of finding out that their condition cannot be cured, or that the sex dysfunction is indicative of a marital disharmony that has deep roots. Pessimism about cure is almost always unjustified. The suspicion of discovering a marital disharmony is justified in many cases. But this disharmony will have more chance of being resolved if it is openly faced than if it is denied. Removal of sexual difficulties often brings people closer to their authenticity, and consequently makes them more likely to come within the grasp of love.

9: EQUALITY AND INEQUALITY IN THE LOVE RELATION

MARRIAGE

When the love partners want to add a feeling of lasting commitment and a binding quality to their pairing, they generally seek marriage. Marriage is a special relation between two people of different sex that has been created by society and sanctioned by the law. It is beyond our purpose to discuss the social and legal characteristics of marriage, such things as mutual obligations and rights. We shall take into consideration instead only what is directly related to the love relation. In our present society marriage is expected to be a union that has been motivated by love, permits the gratification of love's desires, and protects and preserves love. No other relation seems to offer so much intimacy, closeness, common purposes, exchange of warmth and tenderness. Together with another relation mentioned in Chapter 2, the marital relation can fully actualize Martin Buber's I-Thou formula. The "I" loves the "Thou" and the "Thou" loves the "I" in a simultaneous interchange. We can add that in this relation ideally our love reflects the other, like two mirrors which face each other, so that each other's reflections continue to be reflected *ad infinitum*. The relation we referred to in Chapter 2 in connection with Buber's formula is the mother-child relationship. But whereas this relationship presupposes a state of inequality, since the child is dependent on the mother, the husband-wife relationship is one of equal interdependence. Equality and difference, or equality and inequality, are conditions to be carefully considered in a marital situation because it is on a proper understanding and evaluation of them that love depends for its preservation. Actually most varieties of these conditions can exist not only in marriage but in any lasting romantic relationship. We shall discuss them in the marital situation, but what we describe could be applied by the reader to other relations, after having made the necessary modifications.

The sexual polarity of the male and the female tends to accentuate the differences between them, but the partners of a couple love each other both because they are different and because they are alike. They are always more similar than different; they are both members of the same species, and they are made for mating and attracting each other.

They are similar and different in many ways. They are similar in having one goal for their lives; they want to have children in common; they want to grow together. They share a common way of thinking and feeling about the important things of life, the basic philosophies of living which are seldom expressed in words but exist as unconscious or semiconscious presuppositions. But they are also two and different, even when they are in sexual union, in the closeness of forming one flesh, in the closeness of the home and family. They are always two independent minds. And rightly so. They must each try to expand the other's views, enlarge the other's horizons, provide what the other lacks, support the other, correct the other, balance the other. *Vive la différence*, as the saying goes, not just in anatomy, but also in the actions of people in love. The male will bring a masculine world view to the union and the female a feminine one. Except for the fact that sex hormones may be partially responsible for making men respond more aggressively than women, the masculine and feminine roles are a product of child-rearing practices and of the sociocultural environment (Maccoby and Jacklin). The family, the school, society at large, accentuate tremendously whatever difference existed in behavior because of hormonal influence. Even though the masculine and feminine roles are predominantly the result not of nature but of postnatal experiences, they cannot be dismissed or minimized. Inasmuch as males and females have been trained since early childhood for a specific role linked to the gender, they have developed some special personality traits, have learned different skills, and have been attuned to experience the world in different ways. It would be difficult for a person to identify with both roles. Each of the partners assumes a stance toward life that is not opposite but complementary to that of the other. The difference in roles, the similarity of basic philosophies of life, the common goals and the common pursuit of happiness, are all elements that nourish and maintain the loving relationship.

Although the romantic idea, cultivated especially in the past century, is only an illusion, that for every individual there is only one person somewhere in the world who will be his perfect match, and that it is up to him to find this person or he will lose his chance, it is also not true that a loving disposition and desire for love should make every human being of the other sex acceptable. A loving attitude is certainly important, but affection and attraction for a specific person are necessary, too. Once the feeling of love is present, it must grow, and it will grow if it is cultivated. Love is also a promise which, in order to be kept, requires a constant redefinition of the relation in the various periods of life and a constant adding to the original affective nucleus and bond.

A successful romantic union is one in which each partner contributes to the development of the other as much as to his own. Some sociologists have stressed what they call homogamy, the fact that partners in marriage frequently resemble each other in various physical, psychological, and social characteristics (Burchinan). They tend to have grown up in the same place, and to have belonged to the same social, religious, and economic groups.

Robert Winch was one of the first sociologists to challenge the concept of homogamy with his theory of complementarity. Winch argued that although it is true that some degree of similarity favors attraction, it also limits the marriage prospects to a "field of eligibility." Within the field one seeks a partner who is unlike oneself, whose qualities will complement one's own.

In our view, as we said earlier, it is not necessary that partners be too similar or too different. The main point is that the partners grow together. What is necessary for the continuation and growth of love is a special form of equality. What we mean is that despite the striking differences in anatomy, role, and, at times, personality, the two partners must maintain equality in what we call marital assertiveness. It is utopian to think that even the partners of the happiest couple are in agreement about everything. As a matter of fact, if it seems that they are, it is because one of the two renounces making choices and at the same time suppresses the awareness of his renunciation. When there is no agreement, each partner must yield to the other approximately 50 percent of the time. Neither partner should feel that he submits to the other, or that in the marital situation inevitably one must retain a superior and the other an inferior role. Unfortunately this state of equality does not exist in many couples or is soon lost, and love is put in a state of jeopardy. What is the reason?

ORIGINS OF MARITAL INEQUALITY

First of all, we must consider that when two or more people, married or not married, related or unrelated, are together, a difference is established in the way they exert their will. Samuel Johnson observed, "So far is it from being true that men are naturally equal, that no two people can be half an hour together, but one shall acquire an evident superiority over the other." The phenomenon exists among other species, too. For example, when two monkeys are placed in a cage, it will soon appear to the observer that one becomes dominant, the other submissive. There may be biological reasons for this; namely, one of the two may be stronger or may have a more alert nervous system. It could also be that the monkey developed either submissive or dominant qualities on account of accidental happenings earlier in life. The fact that animals practice dominance is not proof of its validity; on the contrary, it is for human beings an additional cause to transcend animal status. By opposing these animal traits we do not violate our nature. We inhibit that part of our nature which is still animal-like, and we enhance the part that is specifically human. But it is indeed very easy to fall prey to the desire to dominate even the loved person. The individual must maintain strict vigilance to prevent himself from exerting power over the partner and to prevent the partner from exerting power over him. The reasons for exerting power over others are many. We have already referred to them in Chapter 3; they are related to fear of the neighbor, of a person other than yourself. Here we shall consider what is pertinent to the marital situation. We may divide these reasons into psychological and sociocultural.

From a psychological viewpoint, we can say that even though partners may believe in equality, they may slip into the practice of exerting power when they have that special type of fear which we have referred to many times—insecurity. To accept equality easily means to be secure, because if you are insecure, you are afraid to lose equality. To make sure that one does not lose equal status, he wants to exert power or acquire more power. The insecurity may stem from a low evaluation of one's worth. If one thinks he has little to offer and cannot be accepted as a worthwhile person, he is likely to believe that he will be accepted or tolerated because he is in the dominant position. The dominant position may be retained economically, legally, through prestige or social status, or through various ways of relating in authoritarian fashion. If insecurity motivates one to seek dominance, it motivates another to accept submission in an attempt to avoid punishment, or in the hope that the dominant individual will be placated and not make additional demands.

When there is an association so intimate and demanding as the romantic relationship, the fear may increase. One of the partners protects himself by increasing his power, that is, by taking from the other some power of making choices and of taking initiative, and allocating it to himself. The other partner seeks protection by accepting a subordinate role: "It is up to him to make decisions; it is up to me to follow." She says to herself, "I choose to follow," but she does not really choose. She is generally not even aware that she is afraid not to be submissive. The fact that women give birth to children and nurse them has pre-disposed her to limit any initiative she has to that realm. Whereas in the successful marriage parenthood adds an-other dimension and another possibility of maturation for both parents, in the unbalanced union that we are discussing, parenthood may limit maturation.

Frequently, though less than in past eras, our society has sanctioned a type of union in which the man has a domi-nant, and the woman a submissive, role. Often, after a very romantic beginning in which each of the partners is very considerate about satisfying the wishes and rights of the other, the male gains supremacy. He becomes the leader, the wife the follower. The dominance becomes stronger and the submission grows. If we look below the surface, we see that this disparity, which threatens the growth or continuation of love, is the fear we have referred to: fear on the part of the male and on the part of the female. Society has in certain ways supported these fears by deny-ing that they are fears and by calling them roles.

There is no doubt that sociocultural conditions have contributed to the male's dominant position. Since pre-historic times the woman has not enjoyed equal rights or equal opportunities with men. She has been taught that her natural character is to be submissive. The indoctrina-tion has been so successful that even great men and women have accepted the inequality as both natural and sanctioned by religion. By extending the inequality of position, many have come to regard the differences be-tween men and women as not limited to sexual characteris-tics, voice, skin, muscular development, and strength, but occurring also in the ability of the central nervous system, in intelligence and wisdom. Yet there is no established dif-ference in the brain of a woman and that of a man. If women have not contributed so much to culture as men have, it is because they have not received the opportunity to do so. Virginia Woolf writes in her book *A Room of One's Own* that if William Shakespeare had had a sister with the same potentialities as he, she would not have gone very far. Even if by chance she managed to secure an education and wrote plays, these plays would never have been heard, printed, or performed.

Since women were relegated to the home and the kitchen, they could not develop their potentialities; they nevertheless were blamed for their lack of achievement. It was respectably said that they did not have the same capabilities as men. The "natural function of a woman" was thought to be working in the home and caring for children. The alternative was to be a dependent old maid, a condition considered disgraceful. Schopenhauer, the pessimist philosopher, considered women definitely inferior to men. Freud accepted their passive role as inherent in the biology of woman's psyche, and the eminent Freudian psychoanalyst Helene Deutsch made the statement that "a deep-rooted passivity and a specific tendency toward introversion" are typical qualities of the woman. Of course, later on, female analysts who departed from Freud and belonged to the neo-Freudian schools protested against such appraisal. Among them are Karen Horney, Clara Thompson, Natalie Shainess, and Ruth Moulton.

It is absurd to maintain the thesis that the inequality of woman's position is justified on the ground that she is suited only for housekeeping and motherhood. After the Industrial Revolution, women were hired as factory workers. According to Engels, in 1839 only 23 percent of the factory workers in England were men. Many women had to work up to sixteen hours a day for salaries far inferior to those received by men. Marx, Engels, and Lenin examined the inequality to which women were subjected and became advocates of women's rights. They considered women's subjugation to be a product of bourgeois society. Capitalism, they said, defends a patriarchal society that permits the preservation of property and the transmission of it from one generation of males to the next. Yet after the success of communist revolutions, communist society, after a very brief period of women's emancipation, returned to the traditional practice, even when Lenin was still in power. In Russia today, women have a position in politics, science, and literature much inferior to that of men. Society has already found reasons for justifying or explaining the submission of women, from their alleged intellectual inferiority to the assertion that their nature has developed in them only maternal or housekeeping qualities.

Many men take for granted the dominant position; they believe it to be their natural right. They allow union with their beloved ones to change from a relationship of equality of right to one in which they sometimes slowly, sometimes swiftly, assume leadership. Often a hierarchy of importance is not only established but openly acknowledged. After all, the man goes to work, earns the money, acquires greater experience of the outside world, while the wife stays home. It seems natural to him that he be the boss in the family. Whereas the man pursues his career, something which means a great deal to him and which he finds fulfilling, the woman must devote herself entirely to the house. Whereas love, affection, and warmth are supposed to be equally given and received, the distribution of things to be accomplished by each of the spouses is very unequal. Although the husband depends on the wife for many needs, generally these needs (like making the bed, making sure that there are eggs, butter, and milk in the refrigerator) do not receive the same consideration as going out in the world and bringing back economic security and status. Thus the relation of mutual dependency becomes more and more asymmetrical. Moreover, as Lerner has stressed, men are generally reluctant to acknowledge their dependence on women for gratification of reputed inferior needs and therefore suppress the awareness of it.

What is required of men is not to participate in the inequity that women have suffered with historical and societal sanctions. It is no longer plausible to say that what has existed for thousands of years must have a certain validity; archaeologists and anthropologists teach us that human beings have pursued some absurd practices for at least 20,000 years. Many men are doing their best to remedy the situation. They sincerely believe that such inequality is unfair; nevertheless, a discrepancy remains between their belief and their behavior. Without being aware of it, in their general attitude toward their wives, they continue to expect acts of submission from them. Thus, as we already expressed, they must maintain a constant vigilance and a desire to correct their habits.

Ruth Moulton has pointed out that although "rapid social change is an outstanding characteristic of our times," the norms, mores, conventions, and traditions that regulate the relations between men and women continue to have an effect on our psyche. "The unconscious tends to lag behind, reflecting the past as well as the present." Not only are men slow to change their attitudes toward women; women, too, are slow to change their attitudes toward themselves. According to Moulton, "The unconscious of modern woman contains many remnants of the conscious misconceptions of her grandmother." In other words, women are prone to accept the unequal position.

CONDITIONS OF INEQUALITY

At times it is difficult not to fall into situations where one dominates. In some cases in which the husband is prominent in some field—politics, science, literature, art, business—the woman is considered simply his wife. She even loses her status as a person and becomes only a satellite or an appendage of the great man. It is understandable that in such cases people may pay more attention to the husband than to the wife. It must be the constant aim of the husband, however, to demonstrate with his actions and feelings that she is just as valuable as he is. The wife must realize that her personal worth is neither decreased nor increased by the fact of her husband's prominence. She should feel neither glamorized nor eclipsed by his position. Her genuine worth is increased by the marriage only if she herself grows as a result of it.

We have spoken of situations in which the male partner is the dominant other and the female partner is submissive. There are, of course, many cases in which the opposite situation occurs. The woman is the dominant one, the man submissive. Here the reason for the lack of equality is to be found exclusively in the personalities of the partners, not in pressures generated by society. As a matter of fact, when the male is the submissive one, society is less tolerant of the relation and invests it with an aura of ridicule. The woman is called "a bitch"; until recently the expression "she wears the pants" was used in a derogatory way in reference to many a wife. This expression shows the prejudice of society; only the man should wear the pants. Indeed, the fact that many women today like to wear pants is not just a fashion devoid of symbolic meaning. It is a quest for equality. The situation in which the woman is dominating is no more or less wrong than when the male is dominant. Whoever is the dominant one, the lopsidedness of the relationship is based on the insecurity of the partners. When a relation is based on domination of one spouse and submission of the other, at first there may be on the part of one partner a denial of the inequality and the suppression of resentment. Eventually the hidden fears and hidden tears become visible. The enchantment is replaced by frustration, anger, or by even more devastating toleration and indifference. But eventually there is a collapse of love, and often of the marriage, too.

The question at times is not only one of love and happiness, but of mental health, as a considerable number of people involved in this situation become depressed. Although what follows may occur in both men and women, we shall describe the condition in women, who are affected by it more frequently than men. Some women become seriously depressed after a few years of marriage, frequently even after twenty or twenty-five years. Some of them even become suicidal. Life, they think, is pointless; themselves they consider guilty or hopeless. Because of the danger of suicide, these women are at times hospitalized. The severe depression is the result of the failure of an extremely important personal relation with a person designated "the dominant other." The dominant other may be a person besides the husband, as described elsewhere. Here, however, we shall only consider the numerous cases in which the dominant other is the husband. The woman, generally a compliant person, has relied on the man for support, guidance, affection. She believes that her husband requires a lot, and she is willing to pay the price. She works hard, she follows, she complies, she accepts his ideas, his ways, without fully deliberating whether these are really worthy of her consent. She does not listen to her wishes; she accepts her husband's wishes and believes they are her own; soon she loses the ability to wish altogether.

The dominant other does not necessarily dominate her life, but he has come to play the dominant role in her mind. The dominant other provides his wife with the evidence, real or illusionary, or at least the hope, that acceptance, love, respect, and recognition of her human worth are acknowledged by at least one other person. But sooner or later (at times, very, very late—even decades after) she realizes that by this relationship her life and personality have been impoverished rather than enriched. She has paid too high a price. If the man required so much and gave so little in return, was he really worth her love? And what kind of love was it? She realizes, even if she has never expressed her feelings and ideas with these exact words, that if love implies caring about the partner's development as much as one's own, her partner's love was not real love. Thus the realization comes that she has devoted her life, or an important part of it, to a relation that was not worth the sacrifice. The result is depression, at times moderate and easily remedied, at others severe and requiring much medical attention.

The two partners may actually come together because of their insecurity, mistaking this insecurity for love. It is because of his insecurity that a dominant person selected a submissive one and a submissive one accepted a dominant one. The two feel bound to each other; they feel that their relationship is based on love, not insecurity. The relationship may last, but only because of the fear each has of being alone. This fear is so strong that they will accept the most undesirable conditions. Some women have not asked to marry their single lovers because they fear that if they mention marriage, their lovers will give them up. Other women remain tied to undesirable persons because they fear loneliness or not being able to find anybody else who will appreciate them. Some men remain married to repeatedly unfaithful wives because they fear that no one else will accept them. We almost always find a paradoxical situation: the dominant partner may seem to remove the insecurity of his partner, but actually exploits the insecurity in order to perpetuate the situation that is advantageous to him; he may give the impression of reassuring, but it is a superficial reassurance and has strings attached to it. Taking advantage of someone else's insecurity is an exercise in power, not in love. A relation based on fear should not be maintained. The person, with professional help if necessary, must find the origin and sustaining force of the insecurity. Such persons, liberated from their fears, will be able to proceed more easily toward love.

We must clarify one point. Dependency and insecurity on the part of one partner (generally female) do not necessarily indicate lack of love on the part of that partner. As a matter of fact, she may feel that being insecure, dependent, needing protection, are characteristics of her being in love. She may become more and more submissive, incapable of being on her own. On the other hand, the dominant partner may see her only as a person who needs him, and he may not recognize her love or his own needs. He may eventually leave her, with tragic results. This series of events is artistically portrayed in Fellini's classic film *La Strada*. A primitive, brutal man, impervious to love, exploits a poor girl, Gelsomina, who, in spite of being victimized and of not being well endowed mentally, is capable of love, even of loving him. He eventually abandons her. As a result of this psychic trauma and her inability to take care of herself, Gelsomina becomes sick and dies. When by chance the man hears the news of her death, he has a sudden insight. He understands her love, he recognizes his crime. He is struck by remorse, pain, depression, and is overwhelmed by love for her. He finally becomes a man.

These cases are fortunately rare. We should not believe that all relationships originating in insecurity or dependency of one of the partners are destined to fail or end in tragic ways. Not at all. Many relationships and marriages, though complicated by the interpersonal relations that we have described, are yet eventually successful. They go through difficult phases, but the difficulties are not unmanageable. Insecure people do not get married only because of their insecurity. A submissive woman may have been attracted to a domineering man, but she was also attracted by other qualities, such as his intelligence or his vitality. Similarly, the man may have become attracted to the woman not just because she was submissive, but also because she was warm, kind, gracious. With the help of psychotherapy (or self-analysis if the partners are capable of it), a new relation should be built on these other qualities. Even in the practice of domination and submission there are elements of love. These elements have to be cleansed of their vicious appendages so that the relationship can bloom and flourish. But, someone might ask, if the main need in the relationship was to dominate or to be dominated, can the relationship last if the partners achieve equality? The answer is yes, if the partners recognize that these needs are harmful, and if they work hard to overcome them, with or without therapeutic help.

10: LIVING TOGETHER
AND ITS COMMON VICISSITUDES

In normal circumstances the closeness of marriage is a great promoter of personal growth. In the process of living together each spouse reexamines his or her previous ways of doing things and tries to see the rest of the world at least from the viewpoint of another human being, a dear one. Each soon becomes aware of a larger context of purposes. Whereas when they met each other, they discovered a mutuality of interests and strivings, they now realize that they are engaged in a creation of interests and strivings. Yes, love may be blind, inasmuch as it can make a person overvalue the beloved one, but it can also enlarge one's vision. It teaches one to overlook the petty flaws, to smile at the little personal inconsistencies, and to accept each other's frailty, in a general milieu of warmth and grace.

If living together is enriching and beautiful, it is also fraught with difficulties. Marriage, even the best, is not necessarily a solid structure, and may be very fragile. Trying to counterbalance the fragility by relying on the legality of the marital contract is to barricade feelings, to cover the heart with artificial armor. If a person is unable or unwilling to face and solve the difficulties that may arise in a life of intimacy, for such a person intimate life is not the best way of fulfilling the requirements of love.

Many people believe that a marriage that began well will proceed well, possibly for the lifetime of the spouses. Again we must stress that nothing in the marital situation should be taken for granted. Even when marriage was motivated by genuine love, there is no guarantee of life-long happiness. Certainly a good beginning is better than a bad beginning, but it is only a beginning. Like freedom, love must be preserved and cultivated. Complacency is to be avoided.

In Chapter 9 we discussed the difficulties that originate when equality and mutual commitment no longer exist between the partners. But there are many other difficulties that we have to take into consideration. Perhaps we can divide them arbitrarily into two categories, the little difficulties which very frequently occur in the course of living together and the serious difficulties which occur in special cases. This chapter will deal only with common and minor difficulties. We must stress, though, that these difficulties, although not serious, may become so if not properly attended to.

• • •

THE FIRST DIFFICULTIES

People react differently to the first difficulties that occur in living together. In a large number of instances these difficulties are denied, as they may take place even in a general state of apparent happiness and contentment. An effort is required on the part of the partners to discover their faulty mutual cueing. Faulty mutual cueing between spouses is by no means as traumatic as that between mother and infant, which Margaret Mahler has described in situations that lead to severe psychiatric disorders. Nevertheless it retains some qualities of it; and unless corrected, may lead to unpleasant outcomes. Cueing means sending messages or signals that are not obvious, and at times are denied or misperceived. They are often subliminal, that is, they do not reach the level of consciousness unless a great effort is made to become aware of them. And yet even when they are not noticed, they are sufficient to change gradually a climate of love and romance into one of complacency, tolerance, or reciprocal irritability. In another large number of cases almost the opposite occurs. The difficulties are also relatively mild, but inasmuch as there is a marked difference from the preceding stage, during which the partners felt at the brink of ecstasy, or in a state of bliss where every step of life seemed to follow a harmonious rhythm, the contrast is perceived as strident, and its import exaggerated. At times it is experienced as a surprise or even as a shock. Where has the warmth gone, that affectionate, admiring glance, that desirous searching for each other? Where are those eyes that shone with joyful surprise every time they saw each other's familiar face? And why has an edge in the voice replaced that soft, tender, reassuring tone?

Whether the partners feel apparently happy, contented,

or are aware of the strident contrast, they eventually experience tension. This tension is a state of uneasiness, discomfort, increased fatigue, eventually recognized as at least partially resulting from the interaction with the partner. The state of intimacy is broken, and the relationship becomes more similar to the one that people have with others, maybe friends and neighbors, but not with the romantic partner. Although this change may appear not so dramatic to people who extoll love for the neighbor, let us be frank: When romantic love becomes similar to love for the neighbor, romance itself is threatened. The intimate quality that exists between two lovers and separates them from the rest of the world is lost. Especially in our time, the second half of the twentieth century, when a state of alienation, impersonality, or mechanization pervades a large part of our social contacts, romantic intimacy is like a treasure island, to be preserved with any genuine means we are capable of. When one feels a diminishing sense of intimacy, one feels that the barriers that love had demolished are gradually being rebuilt. The loved one becomes somewhat distant, as we said, resembling more the neighbor, or one with whom we assume a state of partial vigilance, a person to whom one still reveals the nakedness of one's body but not the nakedness of the soul.

What often disturbs the atmosphere of love is the reaction to criticism. A mild criticism from the spouse or a little disagreement is often experienced with great pain, much more than if the criticism came from another person. This strong reaction is based on the premise, not consciously formulated but present in our inner self, that one's beloved should express only admiration, tenderness, and approval. If he criticizes a little action of yours, rejection will ensue. He must not notice a pimple on your face, or he may not like you any more; nor must he see a spot on your dress, or he may think you are sloppy. The person who has been the object even of mild criticism feels deeply hurt and is likely to respond with disproportionate irritation or anger, and an atmosphere of tension arises. But, of course, life cannot be devoid of criticism, as human beings generally are not able to see their own weak spots unless helped by a more objective view offered by others. If the person who loves you corrects you, and does so with delicacy and in good taste, and if you carefully observe his ways, instead of reacting with intense emotionality, you will realize that his remarks are meant not to undermine you but to increase your awareness. Because he is so close to you, he feels he can tell you what he thinks without hurting you. His criticism is directed to a minimal part of you—yes, perhaps to the spot on your dress that you have not seen—but he likes and loves the whole of you; he has chosen you of all people, and he is glad he has done so. If he criticizes you often, or if criticism does not consist of isolated instances in an atmosphere of acceptance but prevails in his exchanges with you, then, obviously, you have reason to worry and suspect hostility. We shall discuss this in the next chapter. However, if you cannot allow your partner to criticize you *occasionally*, then you expect that unconditional love that a mother gives to her child, and only when he is a baby.

UNWARRANTED ATTITUDES AND EXPECTATIONS

Expecting to be totally and unconditionally accepted is not the only regressive feature that tends to appear in the course of living together. Another is the request for complete involvement. Romantic abandon is mistaken for complete involvement. It is true that each partner must be intensely involved with the other. The other or what concerns the other must be high up on the list of priorities.

But even the best romantic union cannot constitute the whole of life, and even the best partner cannot replace the rest of the universe. No life is fulfilled if it is dedicated solely to the love of another human being. Such dedication would actually be a betrayal of love, for love cannot flourish or sustain itself in those conditions. To expect that the partner will devote himself or herself entirely to you indicates a condition of narcissism that does not bespeak maturity. There are many other essential commitments and loves in life, particularly those that we have discussed in the first part of this book. For instance, to expect that the spouse will decrease his love for his or her parents is unjustified unless, of course, that love assumes some qualities of marital love or does not permit a normal marital love. As a matter of fact, if we appreciate fully the value of the intimate romantic relation, we are aware that we cannot overload that relationship. What pertains more to parental or filial love, to friendship, to work, should not be judged, accepted, or eliminated only in the context of marital love, but in itself. To believe that requited romantic love will bestow a magic light and an everlasting meaning to everything is not a useful concept. Let us remember that love is beautiful in the larger context of life, where one's whole life is important, and so are the other people and facets of the universe that enable us to respond to love in our own unique way. Although very meaningful and very intense, romantic love in itself is not the meaning of life. But it does give life one of its greatest meanings, one which is generally found if properly pursued.

Even when overloading is avoided, marital love requires intense interchange. The beloved spouse exerts a major influence on one's life. Often one spouse adopts all the ways of the other, becomes the other's follower in the various paths of living, in political points of view, tastes, selections of friends, philosophical ideas. In many cases the spouse who does the following eventually becomes aware of this state of affairs and resents it deeply. This spouse may even believe that the partner is a dominant other, a tyrant who has brought about a state of inequality similar to those that we have described in Chapter 9. The situation, however, is very dissimilar. The leading partner may be more explicit in his or her ways, or more assertive, or clearer in the directions he or she gives to life, but not necessarily inclined to impose them on the spouse. In most instances the spouse who follows does so on account of a type of personality that preexisted marriage. Maybe the spouse who follows did not dare to assert himself or herself in his or her own family, has become afraid of taking initiatives, prefers to go along with others. In some of these cases the spouse did not resent being a follower in premarital life, but in the intimacy of marriage the tendency to follow becomes more prominent and is resented. It may distort his or her vision of marriage and he or she may blame the spouse, whose only fault, if we want to call this a fault, is of not having encouraged the partner strongly enough to take the initiative. People must be aware that in a marital situation, too, we remain an active force in determining our life, in shaping our destiny, in retaining our identity. It is obvious, however, that if a spouse prevents the partner from initiating actions which promote growth and open new horizons, then such a spouse becomes a dominant other, which may bring about resentment. It is not too rare, for instance, to meet husbands who are reluctant to let their wives go to school or to work, even when the children no longer require close supervision.

Earlier in this chapter we stated that early in marriage each partner reevaluates his or her ways of living, but this statement should not be interpreted as accepting blindly or totally the ways of the other. Some special situations stand out, for instance, in persons, generally women, who have married their teachers or their former bosses. After marriage it is easy to retain the previous position. If Elsie has married John, her teacher, she may continue to see him as a teacher after marriage; and John, of course, likes to teach, even Elsie. The situation may become accentuated by the fact that realistically John has many things to teach to Elsie, let us say in history and philosophy. Elsie may permit John to teach her some notions of history and philosophy, even after marriage, but this teaching must remain as a small exchange in the general context of her relation with John. John is the man she loves, an equal partner in the marital relationship.

Intimacy, in the sense that the partner will know the essential or innermost character of the spouse, is frightening to some. This fear may appear in one of two forms, or both. The first form is rather superficial and may be formulated in this way: "If he knows me as I really am, he will not love me anymore." But this fear is generally unjustified. There is nothing to hide. The fear of revealing oneself is generally related to feelings of inferiority that have an irrational origin in childhood. Love requires trust, and trust includes one's beloved accepting his lover's imperfections and changes. As Shakespeare wrote, "Love is not love/ Which alters when it alteration finds." Moreover, we must realize that intimacy between husband and wife does not mean a necessary elimination of privacy. Even husbands and wives may have their own little secrets, their private worlds, their little areas of embarrassment. It is folly to expect absolute openness and sharing. A person, however, is not entitled to secrets that, if known to the prospective spouse, would prevent the marriage. Nor are married persons entitled to be secretive about matters that are of concern to both partners. Intimacy requires knowing the basic feelings, ideas, principles, philosophies, of the person one loves, but does not mean knowing the totality of the other person. This leads us to understand the other and more profound fear, which only a few people experience and even fewer are able to verbalize. A spouse may believe that the partner has penetrated his or her private world so much as to have obtained a total vision of the way he or she sees the world, and may thus feel entirely possessed by the partner. Ultimate separateness seems destroyed, fusion with the knowing partner seems to have been achieved, but not that beautiful fusion portrayed by mystical theories of love. It seems a fusion or a union that has eliminated one's individuality, autonomy, uniqueness. Such fear is unjustified. What appears as a threat is not intended, nor is it realizable. If you love a person, you want that person to remain a separate person in the world, not a part of you. You may have insight into how your beloved feels and thinks, but you cannot understand him or her fully or see him or her as a transparent entity. If you were able to do so, you would not be you, but you would have become your partner, another center of consciousness, another life. To live the experience of another person in its uniqueness is equivalent to becoming the other.

In some cases a person fears intimacy because of a belief that knowing the other person well, knowing what to expect from the beloved, will lead to boredom. The ability to predict or to anticipate what the other person will say or how the other person will act is seen to be the same as monotony. But predictability on some basic principles or directions of life is reliability, and it is a good trait. To fear lest intimacy lead to boredom and monotony is a denial of human possibilities. We have already stated that it is impossible to know another person completely and fully. The other person remains another person, another nervous system, another heritage of thousands and thousands of previous generations, another mixture of chromosomes, another way of thinking and feeling, another source of unpredictable choices.

SOME MARITAL HABITS AND TENDENCIES

There are other points that we have to consider, as they frequently become matters of concern even in marriages that started well. First of all, we must stress that there is nothing wrong when the husband and wife together are at times referred to as a "couple" and seen as constituting a unity; the couple is more than the sum of two parts. If, however, the identity of the "couple" replaces the individual identity, difficulties sooner or later arise. As we have already said, a partner may at first welcome such an identification, but eventually will be resentful. People want to be themselves and not just the spouse of another.

We have already mentioned that marriage, as a meeting of minds, is a great remedy against loneliness. We must, however, clarify a point that is easily misunderstood. Eliminating loneliness by marriage does not mean giving up the right to be alone. Even the happiest married person needs time to meditate, to be in touch with himself or herself, to be oblivious of the environment, and to hear the voice of the inner self. A marriage that does not permit occasional solitude is not propitious to growth of the individual, and, therefore, to the growth of the capacity to love.

On the other hand, a marriage that does not permit exchanges with the environment is not healthy either. In fact, a danger of marriage is that it will insulate the couple's lives. As the couple becomes more and more self-sufficient and, in sociological terms, becomes the nucleus of the nuclear family, marriage may become the symbol of restriction; all friendships and outside interests may be sacrificed for the sake of a cohesive bond with the spouse. Togetherness comes to mean isolation from the world. The dependency of the spouses on each other gradually creates an exclusiveness that leads to impoverishment of life. What was once conceived as the fulfillment of a love dream becomes a process of erosion and devitalization. People in these situations have described marriage as a prison, a nunnery, an institution, a retreat.

Both partners must therefore do their best to keep the channels of life open, to permit growth in the individuals as well as in the couple. Each spouse must have his or her own interests and friends in addition to their mutual interests and friends. If the wife is a lawyer, the husband should not feel obligated to meet only lawyers and their spouses. If the husband is a teacher, the wife should not be obligated to meet only teachers and their spouses. Individual growth will also promote growth of the couple, as the partners share with the other the result of their growth. Our advocacy of outside interests should not be misinterpreted as a recommendation for an extroverted type of life that has no time for inward reflection and meditation.

Some human beings, married or not married, are afraid of what they do not know and therefore become reluctant to try new ways and new things. They often reduce their life to a few habitual patterns; but human existence is impoverished when unusual steps are never taken. When living is closed to new horizons, marriage focuses on the little unavoidable contingencies that cannot be avoided, the routine complaints—one spouse's snoring, another's perspiring, and so on. Trivialization of marriage is not a necessary outcome of intimate life, and can be avoided by a creative attitude that searches for the new and the unexpected.

The isolation of the couple from the rest of the world is often caused and perpetuated by jealousy, that is, by the desire to keep the spouse as the exclusive possession of oneself, not simply to secure sexual fidelity, but to keep one's hold firmly over the other. Jealousy may have many causes. It may be the result of general insecurity; one fears that the spouse will meet a better person or a better lover and will run off. Other cases of jealousy have been described by Freud; the "third party" or the presumed "third party" is a symbolic representation of the father for the boy, of the mother for the girl. In other words, the fear of the third person revives the old Oedipal conflicts of childhood. Other types of jealousy are more complicated and may be a mechanism of projection that, at times, may reach paranoid proportions and require psychiatric treatment. A husband accuses his wife of being or wishing to be unfaithful; he is not convinced by the wife's protestations and assertions of her innocence. In these cases, the husband himself wishes to be unfaithful but he cannot accept this wish in himself; it would be too injurious to the image he has of himself as the impeccable husband. Thus he keeps the wish out of his consciousness, but the wish returns to consciousness after it has been displaced or "projected" to the wife. He imagines that it is the wife who has such wishes. Of course, the same mechanism may occur in either of the partners.

A special situation in some stunted marriages occurs when one of the partners is able to grow and the other is not, or at least not at the same speed. Either the husband or the wife may grow more, but, statistically speaking, it is usually the husband who does. It is common for the husband's development to outstrip the wife's when the wife has spent many years raising a family. During this time she was confined to the home, while her husband was pursuing a career in the world. We must repeat here what we have stated in this and earlier chapters: If love is to be preserved, both partners must have opportunities for growth.

Again, if there is no possibility of growth for both partners, marriage is not a fulfillment of love, but is a restrictive, demoralizing imprisonment. Parasitism, in the sense of one of the partner's living at the psychological expense of the other, or symbiosis, in the sense of both partners' finding sustenance or worth only in the other, can develop. But as we have tried to show in this chapter, these are conditions that can be completely avoided by considerate and sensitive partners.

11: MARRIAGES IN TROUBLE

MARITAL PROBLEMS AND THE THIRD WAY OF DEALING WITH THEM

We shall deal now with problems that are more complicated than those mentioned in the previous chapter. The marriages we are discussing now were always on shaky foundations, but their instability was often not recognized until the relationship became obviously unsatisfactory.

Often the reasons that brought people together or strongly influenced the seeming completely free choice of the partners are the same that, unless corrected, will eventually bring about difficulties and even the dissolution of the union. We are referring to hidden neurotic conditions of which the spouses had no awareness at the time of courtship, engagement, or even during the first phase of marriage. There are particular cases where specific neurotic needs enhance a pairing that at first seems appropriate but later appears to be only a futile attempt to solve personal problems.

In the simplest cases it is the basically different personality of the partner that brings about first the attraction and then the difficulty. We have already mentioned in Chapter 9 that a person with a dependent personality is attracted to a domineering, aggressive person, who already during courtship takes all the initiatives. In the same way, a domineering, aggressive person is attracted to a submissive person who allows the other to exert power. Problems arise when the inequality in marital assertiveness brings about resentment and unhappiness. But there are many other cases in which the difference in personality, although at first an incentive for the establishment of the relation, becomes the cause for its gradual disintegration. A common case of this kind is found in a couple in which one partner is an extroverted person, interested in things outside the self, always prone to make social contacts and to become absorbed in external life, while the other partner is a definitely introverted person, mainly involved in personal thoughts and feelings, reticent about making social contacts. In the beginning it was the effervescent, nonaggressive qualities of the extrovert that overcame the reticence of the introvert and made possible the establishment of the relationship. Later, however, when the partners have to face life together, they realize that they do not have the same desires or patterns of living. One wants to live a life of action and social relations, the other a life of thought and inner experiences.

Another difficult pairing consists of a partner who is expansive and craves affection and of another who is emotionally aloof, distant, or even detached to some degree. At first the aloof person responds very favorably to the partner who is solicitous in the eagerness for affection. Later, when the expansive person needs an exchange of affection, the aloof partner becomes scared, withdraws more, and difficulty starts.

Some individuals become repeatedly involved, engaged, or even married to partners who are sick, mentally or physically. They are seemingly motivated by love; they want to do the utmost for the sick partner. Strangely enough, once the partner is recovered, reasons are immediately found for dissolving the relation. After the dissolution, the person becomes involved with another who is sick. It is obvious to a therapist that in these cases the individual is compelled to seek a sick partner and to reject him or her when he or she recovers. This neurotic compulsion may have different causes. It may go back to an Oedipal attachment for a parent of the opposite sex who was sick. It may be, too, that the individual is guilt-ridden and can accept love only when it requires atonement.

A common type of union is the one determined by the "savior complex." Generally the male partner, but occasionally the female, too, wants to rescue the loved person from an unbearable situation, from cruel parents, from poverty, from a terrible husband or wife, from a psychopathic fiancé. In many of these cases, we recognize typical Freudian Oedipal situations. The partner who wants to save used to nourish fantasies as a child of how to save or console the mother, who was harassed by the misdeeds of the father. The savior now tries to fulfill his dream. Sometimes in saving the partner the savior tries to save the neurotic, or fallen, part of himself, and in doing so he derives self-gratification. He believes he is great for having saved another person. A deep feeling of inferiority may be at the bottom of this savior complex. "Only if I save her," he says to himself, "will she love me. I am not worthy of love under any other circumstances." Or he may believe that he can only obtain gratitude, not love. When the woman is the savior, she generally wants to rescue the male partner from a terrible woman, or from a vice, like drinking, gambling, drug addiction, mental illness, or even criminality. Since in most cases no saving takes place, the relationship continues. In the few cases in which the male partner really changes and loses the bad trait, the relation is likely not to continue. The female partner no longer has the mission on which her love was based, and looks for another person who needs her.

Often difficult to distinguish from the person who wishes to be a savior is the person who seeks and finds a state of resignation. The partner who has married a person who is by far inferior in mental or physical qualities, or who is deemed inferior because of being much older or in a lower social class, or in an ethnic group which social prejudice considers less desirable, may suffer from a "resignation complex." Real love, he or she thinks, can overcome all differences. In fact, the privileged partner professes love for all humanity and freedom from prejudice. In some instances such is really the case; unfortunately, however, in many cases these considerations are only a veneer. The privileged partner has made an act of resignation, and simply does not expect anything better.

Almost opposite the marriage of resignation is the marriage of ambition. The partner chooses a spouse because of his or her prominent position. In some cases the partner who is consciously motivated by ambition marries one who is unconsciously motivated by resignation. If the partner with the prominent position is a woman, she is sought by a man who has traits typical of the so-called prince consort. If, on the other hand, the woman seeks a man in prominent position, and is consciously motivated by ambition, she may find herself with problems she did not anticipate. Whereas her husband may still suffer the savior complex, or have the idyllic vision of a prince who has married a little peasant girl, she may be trying through her husband to satisfy her infantile wish to be a man. When her husband resents her assuming "a masculine role," conflicts will ensue.

In a relatively common type of couple, a partner unconsciously searches for and finds a spouse who will fulfill a maternal role. Generally the partner wants a spouse who acts like a mother, either because the mother he had did not fulfill the maternal role, or, because he has not yet been able to outgrow a very marked dependency on his mother. A spouse who is very willing to supply maternal love freely and almost unconditionally, at first seems very desirable to the partner. Later on, however, when the partner realizes that this spouse does not offer sufficiently what is to be expected in a mature relation between adults, serious problems arise.

The list of unstable or neurotic marital unions could be continued at great length. In the next section of this chapter we shall discuss a common type characterized by hostility. At this point we want to indicate, however, that when the spouses are in a marital relation that started well and gradually became an unhappy one, they are prone to envision only two possibilities for dealing with the situation. One of them can be defined with such words as resignation, acceptance, submission, making the best even of relating to a very incompatible person. The other possibility is dissolution of the unhappy union through separation or divorce. Certainly divorce is to be accepted when everything else has failed. Unless prevented by religious scruples, legal customs, or other special considerations, each person feels entitled to pursue love again after an unsuccessful and painful attempt.

Every person who is unhappily married, however, should be aware of a *third* possibility: searching for the reasons that brought about the marital difficulty and studying the possibility of remedying the situation through understanding and a determined effort to change some patterns of living. Just as delaying treatment for a physical illness complicates therapy, so failure to correct marital problems in the early stages may lead to greater difficulties later. Marital problems, however, can also be remedied later in life, although a greater effort is required. Fear of saying or admitting the truth certainly is not conducive to the solution of problems. *Even the recognition that love is based on a neurotic premise and that the apparently free choice of a marital partner was largely motivated by neurotic conditions does not necessarily mean that love is impossible and that the marriage has to be dissolved.* Even a choice largely motivated by neurosis is not completely unfree. There is always a margin of freedom in every choice, and, as we said earlier, real qualities were likely taken into consideration, too, in the choice of mate. These qualities have to be stressed, fortified, and relied upon for the rebuilding of a new and healthier relationship.

Many marriages that originally took place because of a neurotic motivation finally develop into wonderful unions characterized by love and harmony. Even some cases where the savior complex or the resignation complex incited the marriage, instead of detracting, it added to the marriage, after a full understanding of the relation took place. Although one partner married to rescue the other, or because the other was inferior, the rescue really took place, the inferiority really was eliminated, and the ground prepared for the flourishing of love. In still other cases, the sick, even psychotic, partner was not abandoned once he or she recovered. On the contrary, the new understanding of human nature and its predicament, obtained during illness and recovery, added new dimensions to their mutual awareness and more solid ground on which to make their love grow. Even a marriage resulting from unhealthy ambition can be rescued. For example, in one instance a beautiful woman who, as she herself put it, "sold herself" to a rich older man, was very unhappy. After a while, her treatment led her to discover her own feeling of inferiority which obligated her to sell her beauty. This discovery made in its turn possible the discovery of the inferiority of the husband, who could only "buy" love. Once these barriers were destroyed, these two people were able to start a new relationship based on love.

Even marital unions of partners with opposite types of personality are susceptible to correction and are not necessarily destined to fail. If John, an extrovert, married Joanne, who is an introvert, their marriage was certainly facilitated but not exclusively determined by the polarity of their personalities. John could have married Marie or Josephine, who are also introverted; and Joanne could have married George or Theodore, who are also extroverted. Similarly, if Elizabeth, a lady craving affection, became involved with Louis, a rather detached individual, and not with Tom or Dick, who are equally detached, other causes participated in the bringing about of these unions. We must stress once again that in all these cases the partners should not concentrate on the basic differences of their personalities; they must develop further the additional characteristics and rely on them for a compatible union. At the same time they must endeavor to modify or control the extreme manifestations of their basic personality, meet on a middle ground, and increase the pool of love.

One of the mentioned combinations, however, is more difficult to solve and may require prolonged therapeutic intervention. We are referring to the couple that consists of a partner who at first needed maternal love and a partner who at first had the need to be maternal. The difficulty lies in the fact that the partner who requires maternal love is afraid of breaking the relationship, since he has very strong dependency needs. Even this situation, however, is not beyond repair.

As we mentioned previously, if a couple has really been able to solve—not just to cover up—marital problems, the life of the partners will acquire unpredictably positive aspects. These originally unhealthy but ultimately successful unions may, in certain respects, be compared to some works of painters, musicians, or writers which, though motivated by neurotic conflicts, are beautiful creations. We can also add that a marriage that has successfully solved its difficulties has gained in strength.

HOSTILITY IN MARRIAGE

Several extremely difficult situations, like that of being married to a partner who is an alcoholic, a drug addict, a psychopath, or repeatedly unfaithful, will not be considered in this book, as they require prolonged studies of various kinds as well as intensive therapy. In this section we shall discuss only that difficult marriage which is characterized by hostility. Hostility, of course, is not a characteristic exclusively of some marriages; as a matter of fact, it may occur in any type of interpersonal relation. It may be experienced by one person for another, or by two or more persons for one another, no matter whether they are parents and children, siblings, relatives, friends, strangers. We shall limit our discussion, however, to hostility as it appears in the marital situation.

First of all, we must ask: What is hostility? It is a feeling or an attitude, generally based on anger, which tends to elicit a behavior that harms or hurts another person or a group. When the behavior constitutes physical violence, hostility is generally called aggression. Although physical violence does occur in some marriages and is easily brought to the attention of people on account of its manifest results, legal involvements, and newspaper reports, it is, statistically speaking, the least frequent type of marital hostility. This special type will not be considered in this book.

What we shall discuss instead is the hostility that harms in less evident ways.

A simple form of hostility is characterized by coldness, withdrawal of affection, diminished communication. Expressions of praise and endearing terms are no longer used. A common form of hostility is manifested by a marked critical attitude toward the spouse. We have already mentioned in Chapter 10 that occasional criticism on the part of a marital partner does not necessarily indicate a negative disposition but may be an expression of the human desire to help the dear one. In these cases the evidence of affectionate concern negates the intent to hurt. When the spouse, however, showers the other with criticisms, one after another, in various activities of life, even the most minute, the effect is certainly not improvement, but inflicting on the other a loss of self-esteem. The critical spouse may insist that his only aim is that of helping the partner and may even convince himself that he is very useful in this respect, while the other suffers in anguish and humiliation. In quite a few cases the criticism is a power maneuver. If the critical spouse becomes the acknowledged wiser partner, he may have his way all the time. The desire to hurt rather than to help is evident when the global acceptance of the criticism would mean to change completely one's personality and become a shadow of the partner. This actually implies rejection on the part of the partner of the way the spouse is.

At times the critical partner experiences what can be called an irrepressible drive to perfect the spouse; but inasmuch as nobody could be perfect, the criticism is interminable. At times the hostile person resorts not to obvious criticism but to ridicule or mocking, contemptuous behavior, even when friends or acquaintances are present. Again he may insist that he is only humorous, funny, that he jokes, but actually what he expresses is demolishing sarcasm. In fairness to him, in many cases he is not aware of what he is doing. He may be in good faith when he claims that he is only humorous, or when he states that the spouse has no sense of humor. Even so, if he really had no intention to hurt, he would stop using a type of humor when he has realized that the spouse cannot take it and is obviously hurt. He could easily prove that love and affection are more important to him than the retention of his usual "humor."

Another way of discharging hostility is by contradicting the spouse incessantly, even when the differences of opinion are minimal and could be easily overlooked. A partner may also display hostility by changing his or her behavior in ways that displease the spouse, for instance, by keeping company with undesirable people, gambling, having sexual escapades, by going on vacation alone, wasting money, becoming stingy, doing exactly the opposite of what is expected, and so on. Another form of hostility consists of repeatedly and unnecessarily making statements that disturb the partner because of his or her values, religious convictions, political ideas, tastes, and so on, or, even more frequently, by talking adversely about people dear to him or her—parents, aunts or uncles, cousins, friends, colleagues. Needless to say, each partner is entitled to his or her own views on these matters, and is entitled to express them, but should do so with finesse, consideration, in appropriate circumstances, and not for the purpose of hurting. Particularly painful are remarks that imply the spouse's sexual inadequacy. One woman used to manifest her hostility by revealing to her husband dreams in which she had satisfactory sexual relations with other men. These revelations were made under the pretense of honesty and sincerity. In another instance, a husband manifested hostility by revealing to his wife that he had to have fantasies about other women in order to experience pleasure during sexual intercourse.

It is inappropriate to brand the hostile spouse as a malevolent creature and to do nothing about it. That in many cases he is not malevolent, in spite of the sorrow he causes, can be determined by one of these two facts or both: (1) he is not even aware that he is hostile; (2) if he recognizes that he is hostile, he does not know the causes of his hostility. He is usually very skillful in finding reasons for justifying his attitude and often he sounds convincing: the others are wrong, *they* need correction, *they* misunderstand him, do not appreciate his humor, his needs, his rights, his self-assertiveness. These are, of course, rationalizations, often based on pretexts or on occasional grains of truth. The major truth is that he is so busy demonstrating or defending his alleged righteousness or superiority that he cannot reach the inner sources of his conflicts and the secret motivations of his behavior. In some cases the hostility is no longer disguised as a desire to help, to be honest or humorous. It is openly acknowledged as a desire to insult, belittle, demoralize. In cases in which both partners are or have become hostile, the spouses sometimes seem to have lost the capacity to communicate at all, unless they insult each other. Couples of this type are often portrayed in contemporary plays, which unfortunately are realistic representations of a segment of our society. Noel Coward's play *Private Lives* depicts a couple in which the husband and the wife cannot relate to each other except through hostility and violence. Their relationship is built upon a series of verbal and physical battles. In Albee's well-known play *Who's Afraid of Virginia Woolf?* a husband and a wife relate only with unrestrained, brutal hostility. In these plays the spouse, who is expected to be one's most cherished and loved person, becomes the *lupus* we referred to in Chapter 3. This absolute reversal in roles shows fully the tragic nature of these situations. When a play represents comically this form of relatedness, the comic dimension, in addition to its aesthetic aims, becomes a desire to make the audience accept the unacceptable, not as a form of life, but as something which has to be observed and meditated upon so that we can learn to avoid it.

What appears as comic on the stage is disastrous in life. When the hostility exists on both sides, and increases as a reaction to each other's hostility, the marital picture is serious indeed. Divorce may become a necessity. What is even worse, in some cases the partners do not want to separate, but continue to live together because this is the only way they can intimately relate. This, in fact, is the case in *Who's Afraid of Virginia Woolf?*. In rare cases, the relation of reciprocal hostility acquires paranoid characteristics. The spouses accuse each other of unrealistic intents and distort or misinterpret the actions or the words of the others.

The outcome is more promising in cases in which only one spouse is hostile. What can the nonhostile partner do to improve the relation? First of all, he or she must try to understand the spouse in depth, and not just evaluate or assess the manifest actions, behavior, attitudes. What is behind or beyond them? Why is the partner so unpleasant to be with? Is the partner dissatisfied about the marriage as a whole, discontented about sexual life, without realizing or admitting that it is so? What are the secret fears that have to be changed into the form of anger? Does the hostile spouse see in the partner a reproduction of an important figure of the past whom he hated (a parent, a grandparent, an older sibling, a former spouse or fiancé)? Is he ready to fight, because he is easily hurt, because his insecurity makes him always expect to be hurt? Is he so discouraged about himself that he can find sustenance only by demolishing others? Is he angry at life in general because of many disappointments or early traumas, so that he now experiences any form of relating as inimical? Does he need to discharge the anger stored early in life, now that the spouse is there as an easy target? Is he unable to stand closeness? Does closeness scare him, so that while he is capable of being a good friend, he cannot be a partner in an intimate relationship?

The nonhostile partner should deal with the spouse not by fighting and acting defensively, but by trying to explain and to understand, by offering alternatives, by referring to the past as a cause of what happens in the present. The hostile partner, too, can help the situation in some cases if he succeeds in reflecting upon his own attitude. Even if he does not realize that he is hostile, he must ask himself why the spouse experiences him in that way. The fact that other people, like friends or acquaintances, do not recognize that he is hostile, is not convincing proof that he is not. He may be hostile only to persons close to him; perhaps even only to persons whom he loves. As a matter of fact, he may remember that in the past he was also hostile to his parents, for whom he had strong affection. Perhaps early in life he had to pay too big a price for love (submission to a neurotic father, to a despotic mother, to a preferred sibling) and now closeness makes him angry. The hostile partner may come to understand that closeness makes him unconsciously expect that he has to pay a big price again, perhaps loss of freedom, giving up his will, or the like. In some other instances, he may realize that closeness stimulates hostility in him for other reasons: only to people very close to him can he discharge his anger caused by his frustrations in life.

In some interpersonal relations, marital or nonmarital, the hostile individual discharges unwarranted hostility toward another person only. As a matter of fact, if he marries a second time, he may not be hostile to the second spouse, whereas he was to the first. In these cases we must recognize that although the prerequisites for hostility existed, close contact with a partner who had special characteristics was necessary for the hostility to emerge. In other words, what we want to indicate is that although a person may be easily recognized as being hostile toward his spouse, we should never evaluate him in himself, but in the context of the interpersonal relation in which the hostility is manifested.

Many well-intentioned people can help themselves by evaluating all the factors that we have mentioned. Unfortunately, as we have already stressed, in many cases the reasons for hostility remain unconscious, the hostile person continues to focus on his rationalizations, and the person who is the target of hostility is concerned only about how painful it is to be so unfairly and so repeatedly victimized. Marital therapy, that is, a therapy consisting of sessions in which both husband and wife are present and treated by the same therapist, is helpful and recommended in mild or even moderate cases. In cases in which the hostility is very pronounced or very difficult to understand in its origin, both marital therapy and individual psychotherapy are indicated. In the clinical experience of the senior author, in approximately 50 percent of marriages characterized by severe hostility, psychotherapy can bring either solution of the difficulties or great improvement. Even in formerly hostile marriages love can be found.

12: LOVE'S EXPECTATIONS

Is it unwise to expect too much of romantic love? Is love an unexpected occurrence, an inspired moment rather than a permanent state? Is a declaration of love an ill-considered commitment one is not capable of? Is romantic love a mad confusion in people who really seek the other types of love we have discussed in this book? Is love a trick of nature to insure propagation? Does love make the heart young again and cancel the years? Does love enable us to accept the temporality of life? Is love an intense liking of charm rather than an embracing of intimacy and beauty? Is love only a wildly poetic conception?

Let us repeat our first question: Is it unwise to expect too much of love? We would answer with a qualified no. We ought to expect much from love and we ought to prepare ourselves for its realization. These expectations, however, must necessarily include an active participation. If we remember that love is neuropsychologically a complex functional system which involves a tremendous number of neuronal contacts, love's potentiality for growth surpasses what a human being can achieve in his lifetime. The search and the cultivation of love always confront individuals with new situations for which there are no ready solutions. Obtaining a love object is not the end; and one's prospects should not cease there. The individual must find ways to preserve and increase his love. Moreover, consciously or, as is more usual, unconsciously, the individual compares his state of love with his state before his love was obtained, and he appreciates the improvement. But the building of love never ends. He wants to add to it, and he continues the search. By "search," of course, we do not mean the search for other partners. This kind of search is a common neurotic device to avoid the apparently difficult task of adding to the love in the existing relationship.

Philosophers often speak of transcendence, that is, an extending beyond our immediate experience and vision of life. Transcendence is the escape from the mundane routine of life to what is beyond, higher in value, and eternal. When philosophers speak of immanence, they speak of the opposite of transcendence. The purpose of love is to guide the human being to the transcendent world of the infinite, to transform the human being into a creature dwelling in the world of ideas and truth and experiencing unpredictable, elevating feelings. The transcendence will be greater and greater as love informs and fills the human spirit. The purpose of love is to aim the human sight toward the infinite. Put simply, there is no limit to what we can expect from love, but one should not expect love to be enjoyed passively, as we enjoy the sun's rays on a spring day, or as we enjoy the perfumed fragrance in a rose garden. Love can be appreciated, but we must cultivate the garden, we must place ourselves in the rays of the sun.

Some people are disappointed in love. They expect it to be a wonderful gift from heaven—like manna—which just happens, and gives meaning to their lives. After experiencing a period of infatuation, they wait and wait for something good to happen, but it never does; they are waiting for Godot. Many intellectuals have a pessimistic attitude; they see the disintegration of values and ideals, the infectious spreading of materialism and crime, the loss of purpose and faith. Waiting, they say, is futile, too, even as far as love is concerned. But we need not be mere passive puppets whose strings are manipulated by events. The waiting is in vain if we do nothing else except wait. If we are not overwhelmed by the fears of life, as the two derelicts in Beckett's play were overwhelmed, we may find what we seek. Of course, finding one goal does not mean growth should stop. Man will always be *inachevé*, but *inachevé* does not mean unhappy, unloved, unlovable.

Love may begin unexpectedly, in a fleeting moment, at first sight. What is seen in a fleeting moment is like an intuitive vision, a sign of what is hidden and may be revealed later. It is a clue, and it has magnetic power, for it is a clue of love. But the clue does not determine the outcome. Soon those who were intrigued by the first sight will discover whether they can build on what was suggested by the clue.

Is a declaration of love an unthinking commitment beyond one's capacity? There are, to be sure, a small number of people who, because of their psychological or physical makeup, are not able to commit themselves to the demands of lasting love, for love concerns future actions as well as present actions. In this group are included not just psychopaths, but a number of honest, well-intentioned people who are capable only of immediate pleasure. Often they are capable of friendship and social intercourse, but of no relationship more demanding. If these people do not want to change their character, they should not assume the responsibility of marriage or a lasting relationship. Some-times—for instance, in the case of some actors, actresses, and politicians—the only commitment is to a career. For their careers, these people will undergo any type of sacrifice; they are even willing to renounce love.

Sometimes the inability to commit oneself to a love relation springs from a neurotic fear of commitment. The person afraid of marriage is quick with arguments which seem logical, and do have some logical elements in them. Because of their religious convictions, some speak of "the indissolubility of the tie"; others with a touch of humor refer to "a life sentence"; still others mention the unpredictability of life, the uncertainty and danger which attend committing a whole life to a decision of youth. One witty patient remarked, "When I rent a room or apartment, before I sign the contract, I carefully read the lease, even the fine print. But were I to marry and the priest asked me whether I would accept Joan for better or for worse till I die, there is no fine print, no escape clause. Who could write the fine print for what is beyond prediction?" The fine print of marriage cannot, of course, be written down; what is necessary is an attitude of commitment, the desire to assume responsibility for the sake of a very valuable relationship.

Some people believe that marriage is outmoded, and that society must seek other ways to form relations. The trouble is that human beings have not found anything better which is capable of producing intimacy and growth. The people who decry marriage stress its difficulties, but they do not reveal what else would aid the spiritual growth of the majority of people. Some religious individuals may grow more by loving God, others, such as Newton and Kant, by devoting themselves to their work, but the majority of mankind grows by committing themselves to the marital relationship.

Sometimes a person enters a marriage understanding

that a special responsibility is demanded. One should be extremely careful about entering into such a marriage. Even when the emotions surge at the promise of love, one must not give up assessing the responsibilities one is willing to assume. The most common kinds of special demands may be divided into three categories: (1) that one partner accept the ideological or religious views of the other; (2) that one partner take care of the spouse's young children from a previous marriage; (3) that one partner go with the other to live in an outlandish part of the world. If, having accepted one of these demands, the partner fails to live up to it, the marriage may be endangered.

The violating of a fundamental commitment in marriage involves both present and future actions. In most instances, a spouse who very much loves the partner who has broken a fundamental promise makes an effort to understand, forget, and keep the love alive. Such a spouse realizes that for the sake of love the partner promised more than he or she was able to do. In the few cases in which the effort succeeds, the love may even grow after the turbulent crisis. In some cases, the spouse who urged the partner to make that special promise realizes that the urging stemmed from a neurotic imperative. In some other cases the marriage suffers a blow from which it never completely recovers. The spouse who purportedly has accepted the breaking of the promise may harbor some deep resentments. Even after many years he may wake up in the middle of the night and brood over the fact that he was betrayed. He believes that if he urged the partner to make such a promise, it was because that matter had a fundamental meaning to him.

In some cases in which the partners believe that love has not lived up to their expectations, there has been a confusion between romantic love and the other kinds of love. We have already referred to several such cases. For instance, the individual seeks in the spouse another mother or father on whom he can depend for support and guid-

MARRAGE

ance. Obviously, even the best spouse does not want to be a parent to his or her partner. Nor should the spouse be treated like a neighbor. To consider the spouse a neighbor is to make him or her not even a neighbor, but a far, far removed human being. Similarly, one should not try to seek from a love relation the pleasure one finds in work. Some women devote themselves exclusively to maternal love. It is essential that the various loves not be confused. For though one kind of love may contain certain qualities of another (for example, a wife may well exhibit maternal tenderness and parental guidance to her husband), the essential differences ought to be preserved.

There are also other types of love that, although they do not imperil marriage, tend to bring about a limitation of life experiences and ultimately a state of disappointment. These loves are found in what, if we apply Freudian terminology, we can call id marriages, ego marriages, and superego marriages. In each of these cases both partners have a similar outlook toward marital life, but a limited one. In the id marriage the focus is almost exclusively on sex and sensuous pleasure; in the ego marriage the focus is on adjusting in the best possible way to the demands of reality without ecstatic passions or lofty ideals; in the superego marriage, it is on duty, on doing what is expected, on never deviating even minimally from the set goals. Although these unions may lead to contentment, they more often lead to a restricted life. If much is to be expected from love, it must be a love which results from a harmonious integration of id, ego, and superego functions. All the parts of the psyche must be involved in it in intensive ways.

Is love a strong liking of charm and beauty rather than an embracing of intimacy? There is nothing wrong in seeking charm and beauty. Love is beautiful and certainly ought to be embodied in a gracious, charming individual. Indeed, beauty and love are inextricably bound with one another.

The beauty of an individual might not adhere to a fixed standard, say, the proportions of Greek art, but must satisfy the lover. Beauty becomes a symbol which is part of the loved reality—just as a word is a voiced symbol which stands for a thing but may become part of beautiful poetry. As the philosopher Plotinus said, what is beautiful is liked as a message of the invisible through the visible; the visible is a message of the invisible part of love. But the invisible parts of love must become visible as love unfolds. The skin becomes lined, the hair white, the bones frail, but love grants beauty to these, a beauty inherent in the act of love. Thus love cancels the years and keeps the lover young.

Is love a poetic conception? To the German philosopher Friedrich Schlegel, love is poetry and poetry is an analogue of love, an aiming at infinity and God. If we adhere to the view that life is a continuous growing and reaching for transcendence, love enables us to accept the temporality of our life. So long as we have done our best to grow, we can look back on our lives with serenity and peace. The journey of life is an itinerary of love; love may continue to grow without any end.

What began as a fleeting infatuation, based on the visible message of the invisible, has revealed much of what was invisible. Thus love is not to be seen as a coercively, irrationally, indissolubly entered captivity, because a person does not grow in prison, where the mind and the body are both chained. Whoever feels himself in captivity is not in love. Some poets, including the early poets of the Italian Renaissance, have depicted the lover as a prisoner, as a slave of the love object, but these depictions were metaphorical expressions referring to the supremacy of passion. Although artificially beautiful, those poets were not right to see love as a tyrant, and they never achieved the sublime heights of poetry, as the mature Dante did. In Canto 28 of *Paradise*, Beatrice reminds Dante that an act of vision—

that is, an intellectual act—must be united to an act of love to reach beatitude. The will and the desire may have love and beatitude as their goal, but it is the intellect which must apprehend them as good. By *intellect* we do not mean cold analytical intellectualization, but the part of the psyche which consists of ideas, the ideas which bring about the highest emotions. Love, as Milton said, "hath his seat in reason."

If love is allowed to grow properly, it inspires the noblest deeds of human endeavor. From the love for a woman emerged the greatness of *The Divine Comedy*. In this epic of love, Beatrice grows in meaning as Dante's love grows and this love is the symbol of what love can be. Beatrice is the beautiful girl of the emerald eyes, who awakened the heart of the young Florentine; Beatrice is the love which redeems and saves him from the false vision of the good; Beatrice is goodness, and guides the poet to the infinite world which touches the aura of God. In Dante's conception, the growth of love is depicted as a journey of life. In "the middle of the journey of life" Dante finds himself exiled; he is a fugitive wandering from his homeland. But the escape from the dark wood of error, the wandering journey, becomes a journey in search of love. Dante will realize love not in action, but in poetry and wisdom.

Although nothing human is perfect, the poet can conceive of love as perfect. Perhaps given our daily reality the poet is wrong, but artistically he is right, for he promotes goodness and hope, and shows the right direction.

And the poet can make his love immortal (Shakespeare, Sonnet 18):

Shall I compare thee to a summer's day?
Thou art more lovely and more temperate:
Rough winds do shake the darling buds of May,
And summer's lease hath all too short a date:
Sometime too hot the eye of heaven shines,

And often is his gold complexion dimm'd;
And every fair from fair sometimes declines,
By chance or nature's changing course untrimm'd;
But thy eternal summer shall not fade,
Nor lose possession of that fair thou owest;
Nor shall Death brag thou wander'st in his shade,
When in eternal lines to time thou grow'st:
    So long as men can breathe, or eyes can see,
    So long lives this, and this gives life to thee.

PART THREE

LOVE OF LIFE
AND A THEORY OF LOVE

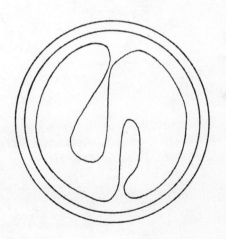

13:   LOVE OF LIFE

Now that we have examined six important loves in human life, let us consider the seventh, which includes all of them, love of life itself.

What is love of life? How can it be defined and interpreted? Does it mean reverence for life? Albert Schweitzer, the Alsatian physician and theologian who spent most of his life treating people affected by leprosy and sleeping sickness in a deserted mission station in the center of equatorial Africa, wrote in moving terms about reverence for life. Schweitzer saw each of us as a life which wants to live, in the midst of life everywhere which wants to live. His ethical conceptions derived from the basic premise that, on the one hand, it is good to preserve and promote life, and, on the other hand, it is evil to destroy, wound, or prevent life. Certainly Schweitzer's concepts are included in love of life, but such a love involves more than an attitude of reverence. And although mature love is ethical, love embraces more than ethics.

Is love of life what the French call *la joie de vivre*? It certainly includes the joy of being alive, the pleasure found in the diversities of an active existence. Generally with these French words we express exuberance and exaltation, but love of life is deeper than rejoicing and exaltation.

Is love of life a state of astonished admiration at this miraculous event in the cosmos, that matter becomes organized into complex molecules, into diversified cellular groupings, into systematized organs which are integrated into one organism which feels, moves, reproduces itself, and, in the human species, is capable of understanding, choosing, and being self-reflective? A scientific view of life can indeed assume a passionate quality and be a part of what we are seeking, but love of life entails more.

Does love of life mean seizing as many as possible of life's pleasures while they are within reach? There is nothing wrong in savoring the pleasures of life, provided we do not infringe upon the rights of others. This does not mean practicing hedonism, epicureanism, or any philosophy of life which focuses exclusively on the enjoyment of easily accessible pleasures which do not depend on our strivings but on our senses, and on what our socioeconomic status makes available for us.

Love of life means to be happy to be born, to rejoice in the functions of life, to be a spectator of the wonders of the universe, and at the same time to be a participant in the actions of the world. It means to be glad that we were made and that in the framework of our limitations, we are also makers. Love of life means also trying to understand life, or searching for its meaning. It means to participate actively in what we know, and to know and feel by participating. Most of all, love of life means accepting and loving all the other loves—love of family, love of fellow human beings, love of oneself, love of work and ideas, love of God and transcendence, and love for the romantically beloved with whom we share every love.

If we say we love life and the blessings life can provide, we mean that we desire to obtain those goods which life offers and to preserve and cultivate those which we already have. When we are speaking of obtaining something, we mean "to take hold of it in the future." Thus if one wishes to preserve his love for another human being, he means that he wishes to continue loving that person in the future. Therefore, love, though it arises in the present and is fully immersed in the present, always tends toward the future; and it is for this reason that lovers, although remembering with joy the past time spent together, always speak more of the future than of the past, for love is at home in our hopes and plans.

When we speak of love of life, therefore, we speak of the desire to live and to preserve life. And this desire really has no bounds. For those who are religious, love of life manifests itself in the desire to achieve eternal happiness, a life everlasting; for those who are not religious, or whose religious convictions do not lead them to ideas of an after-life, love of life means to make the most of life on this earth—to make the most of it in every way, both quantitatively and qualitatively, to live long and well.

For many people, but not for all, love of life reveals itself in the family. For, as Plato wrote in the *Symposium*, most men cannot achieve any kind of real immortality; the way in which they can preserve a part of themselves, in which they can achieve a kind of everlasting life, is by the propagation of children. Thus one's own characteristics are preserved, and in a way in which romantic love is sublimated; for one's characteristics are present in children only in combination with the characteristics of the beloved spouse.

Although we have said that love tends toward the future, by no means do we mean that the past is to be minimized. For there is no better memory than that of a past time permeated by love, especially if that love is still with us. Thus love of life embraces past, present, and future, and includes all other loves.

LACK OF LOVE OF LIFE

Not everybody shares this point of view. People who do not love life actually often hate living or do not consider it worthwhile. Among them we must include some neurotics, some psychotics, some normal but very unfortunate individuals, and even some great philosophers—the philosophers of pessimism, of whom the most famous is Schopenhauer, despised life. Schopenhauer wrote "that we have not to rejoice but rather to mourn at the existence of the world... its non-existence would be preferable to its existence." Schopenhauer believed that it is senseless to speak of life as a gift, as many people, including philosophers, have done. "It is evident that everyone would have declined such a gift if he could have seen it and tested it beforehand." He also stated that the majority of mankind does not obtain happiness. The greatest blessings of life, like health, youth, and freedom, are not appreciated until we have lost them. Perhaps more than by any other consideration, Schopenhauer was driven to his pessimism by what he called the "perishableness" of all good things and the ultimate dissolution of all our hopes and achievements in death. "That which *has been* exists no more; it exists as that which has *never* been.... Hence something of great importance in our past is inferior to something of little importance in our present, in that the latter is a *reality*, and related to the former as something to nothing."

We should not believe, however, that the only people who negate the value of life are the philosophers of pessimism. Disquieting appraisals of life have been made by nonphilosophers as well. Clarence Darrow, the American lawyer and a very compassionate man, famous especially for procuring the acquittal of people charged with killing former Governor Steunenberg of Idaho, for defending Nathan Leopold and Richard Loeb in the "thrill" murder trial, and especially for defending a schoolteacher charged with violating a Tennessee statute that forbade teaching Darwinian theories, wrote, "I love my friends, but they all must come to a tragic end." Life is "not worthwhile. It is an unpleasant interruption of nothing, and the best thing you can say is that it does not last long."

The Russian novelist and philosopher Tolstoy, too, was very pessimistic about life. He wrote that there was no reason to go on making efforts because sickness and death will come to those we love and to ourselves. "Nothing will remain but stench and worms." A good solution is suicide, which, however, can be chosen only by a few "exceptionally strong and consistent people."

And the greatest of all English poets, Shakespeare, tells us (*Macbeth*, Act V, v):

> .... Out, out, brief candle!
> Life's but a walking shadow, a poor player
> That struts and frets his hour upon the stage
> And then is heard no more: it is a tale
> Told by an idiot, full of sound and fury,
> Signifying nothing.

How can we respond to these statements, expressed with sincerity by great men who opened up their souls to us about matters of such grave concern? Let us reconsider the given examples in reverse order. The words of Shakespeare produce a strong impact on us, not just because of the beauty of the metaphors, but also because we sense in them a profound message. Can our life, too, be compared to a brief candle, a shadow, a poor player, a tale told by an idiot? We know that Shakespeare attributes this vision of life not to a hero of love, but to Macbeth, a hero of evil, certainly not a man whom we should listen to as a master of life. Another person might not focus on the shortness of "the candle" but on whatever light the candle could shed, if used for a good purpose. Macbeth's life became possible of definition through those metaphors selected by Shakespeare when Macbeth chose the path of evil and a goal which required betrayal of the human spirit. And yet, since the words of Shakespeare strike us so strongly, we must assume that the poet speaks not only about Macbeth's life, but about the life of all of us, even though we do not commit Macbeth's crimes. The Bard of Stratford-on-Avon tells us that our life, too, can become a shadow, a poor player, a tale told by an idiot—unless we find a meaning in it, and it must be a proper meaning. Macbeth did give a meaning to his life—obtaining power by means of crime—but any meaning discordant with the basic principles of human nature is sooner or later recognized as "signifying nothing." A life dedicated to love and enriched by love acquires the most profound significance.

Tolstoy, after a period of intense self-searching, eventually accepted human love. In *Anna Karenina* he wrote that man is created for happiness, but the happiness depends on him. "Life is everything"; "Life and love are already God." As to Darrow, he spent most of his life trying desperately to save the lives of "the damned." At a time when the death sentence prevailed as a form of punishment for murderers, he defended more than 100 persons charged with murder, and none of them was ever sentenced to death. If he totally believed that the best thing you could say about life is that it does not last long, why did he labor so relentlessly and with so much devotion to prolong a few lives of people who, if they escaped capital punishment, would probably spend most of their remaining years in prison?

People like Tolstoy and Darrow approached the problem of the worth of life with great dedication and sincerity, but nevertheless with their own actions and writings they expressed ambivalent attitudes. When they were discouraged, they responded to the great dilemma with a negative appraisal. But there was no ambivalence in Arthur Schopenhauer. He was an embittered man, a pessimist through and through. A giant of the intellect, he was a dwarf in the realm of love. He attempted to cover the universe of his understanding with the dark blanket of his own unhappiness. He condemned all forms of love inasmuch as they promote the will to live. Inasmuch as love leads to perpetuation of the will to live, it does arouse or should arouse guilt in the lover.

Had Schopenhauer himself been able to experience love, would he have advocated the same ideas? If psychiatric practice teaches something applicable to life in general, and of course we believe that it does, the answer is no. Generally people who despise life are people who were not blessed by family love or were raised in disturbed families, became unable to love others, could not find satisfaction in their work, did not devote themselves to ideals, or if they did, recognized that their ideals were the wrong ones. Most of all, they are people who were not able to find a satisfactory or enduring romantic love. Some of these unfortunate people become very depressed, and a few of them committed suicide or attempted suicide.

The depressed patient who despises life can be greatly helped by a variety of psychiatric treatments. If he undergoes psychotherapy, the psychiatrist makes an effort to understand the origin of the patient's problems, the situations or conflicts which originally warped him and influenced adversely the subsequent stages of his life so that he could not attain the expected satisfactions. If, as a result of the new understanding, the patient becomes capable of changing the patterns of living which tended to perpetuate his depression, he will be able to experience love and hope again, and will love life, too.

Psychiatrists follow general medical practice in aiming to restore health and to preserve and prolong life. Such goals supersede other considerations, so much so that many psychiatrists, when confronted with patients who are very depressed, hate life, and want to commit suicide, are willing to hospitalize these persons even against their will. Not all psychiatrists feel this way, however. The best known of those who dissent is Thomas Szasz, a psychiatrist who strongly feels that no human being should be admitted to a psychiatric hospital against his will. In disagreeing with Szasz, the majority of psychiatrists recognize that it is indeed a very unfortunate step to hospitalize a person without his consent, and that probably the patient, at least as long as his psychiatric condition continues, may interpret this as an attack on his freedom and dignity. The problem is actually more theoretical than practical, because in the majority of cases it is possible to convince a suicidal patient to be hospitalized. A serious problem remains in a hard core of patients who require a long time to be convinced to accept hospitalization, and yet during this period they may make the tragic attempt. If we have discussed this issue at length, it is in order to stress the implied premise in the psychiatrist's attitude that life is such a precious gift that it has to be preserved even at the cost of temporary involuntary hospitalization. In the premise is also included the conviction that in most instances the patient will reacquire love for life once he has overcome his psychiatric condition. This is not to deny that there are instances in which people in good mental health also actualize their belief that life is not worthwhile. In our culture such instances are very rare.

Some philosophers and poets have praised death, which terminates the unhappiness of life. On the other hand, other writers have blamed life because ineluctably it leads to death and therefore brings about the fear of death. The fear of death is so terrible as to make life hard to endure. This possibility, too, is expressed by Shakespeare in *Julius Caesar* in a dialogue between Casca and Brutus in Act 3.

CASCA
Why, he that cuts off twenty years of life
Cuts off so many years of fearing death.

BRUTUS
Grant that, and then is death a benefit:
So are we Caesar's friends, that have abridged
His time of fearing death....

Of course, the person who speaks of abridging the time of fearing death is Brutus, a questionable friend of Caesar, but undoubtedly a person who tries to feel less guilty for having caused Caesar's death. There is an inherent contradiction in those theories which hate life on account of its brevity or because it leads to its contrary, death. These theories implicitly assert that life should be longer and is therefore worthwhile, and preferable to death.

The ideas expressed by Schopenhauer that what counts is only the present, and that past life "exists no more" or "it exists as little as that which has never been" are also questionable. At a human level the nervous system permits us to retain the past as memory traces and to reevoke it spontaneously when the individual wants it. Moreover, the past as an experience becomes integrated in the psyche and becomes part of it. Although it is true that the present and the future are very important and that we should by no means be anchored to the past, our past has become part of us. A person who has lived a rich life does not look with regret at the past or feel as if the past had not existed. The past is still inside of him, is part of what he is now, and he can recall it with pleasure.

Are we not limited by the brevity of our lives, by the tyranny of time? We are. But if we are healthy, we can grow at every period of life. Every age has its beauties and possibilities. Although it is true that the greatest rate of growth occurs in childhood and adolescence, it is also true that most of the profoundest achievements in moral growth, deeds, and thought have been attained by the majority of people at a mature or old age. It is only at a mature age that human beings become sure of their real identity. Moreover, as we have already expressed, the human being is exposed to an increasing number of ideas and concepts, developed in our time or transmitted from previous eras. These concepts, too, become part of us. We may reproduce them as they are or recombine them in multiple, often unpredictable ways. Through language and other symbolic media our nervous system permits us to conceive an infinite number of thoughts and to experience multiple unpremeditated emotions connected with those thoughts. Thus, although we were not their contemporaries, Moses, Isaiah, Jesus, and Francis of Assisi still talk to us and show us the paths of goodness; Homer, Virgil, Dante, and Shakespeare still make us hear their powerful voices; Michelangelo, Leonardo, and Raphael still disclose to us the beauty of their art; Bach, Mozart, and Beethoven still play for us sublime notes; Volta, Galvani, and Edison still put into motion our machines and lighten our homes; and Pasteur and Fleming still protect us from infective diseases. To some extent we can also anticipate events which will occur in the near and distant future.

Thus, this so-called interruption of nothing, this life of

ours, this little window which remains open for a brief period of time, becomes an opening from which we can look at the universe regardless of space and time. We become the spectators of all times and all existences. We become the possible participants in all times and in all existences, because in what we know we participate with our thoughts and our feelings. O window of wonders, if, above all, it lets us see love!

14: A THEORY OF LOVE

Do you remember Professor von Von Kochenbach? We met him in the first chapter of this book. Many people mocked him, because instead of going to the door leading directly to love and paradise he chose to go to a lecture about love and paradise. We know better now, that he made the right choice, that there is no quick route to love. Nor did the old professor end his search for love when the lecture was over. He was not the dusty bookworm that some may have imagined him to be, but a person eager and willing "to seek knowledge like a sinking star beyond the utmost bounds of human thought." He did not recoil at the prospect of learning a little more, just as you, readers, did not hesitate to read this book. He is always searching, always finding, always yearning; he has kept his heart young and cancelled the years. He does not keep his youth as Faust did, by making a pact with the devil, but by making a different kind of covenant, one which instructed him to always aim higher and seek a higher love. No wonder so many young people of both sexes have gathered around him to talk to him and to listen to him. They do not have the feeling that they were waiting for Godot. To some extent they got what they expected—no magic word or magic potion with which to attain love, but a better understanding of how to achieve love. The search, of course, continues. But perhaps a theory of love can now be attempted.

A theory of love can start with anatomy and end with a Dantesque vision, including the cosmos and the divinity as they are presented in the last canto of the *Divine Comedy*. There is a difficulty inherent in the nature of love which makes any theorizing risky, a difficulty to which we have already referred, love's endlessness, the possibility of always adding to it unpredicted dimensions. With these reservations, we can nevertheless make an attempt to formulate a theory, realizing, of course, that other authors can add to it or detract from it and modify it in accordance with whatever new knowledge and new understanding will develop. Our task is made somewhat easier by what we have discussed in the previous thirteen chapters. For each of the seven loves we have examined the origin, the experience, the development, and the decline or loss resulting from adverse circumstances and especially from adverse emotional states, like fear and its derivatives. If we have given particular attention to fear, it is because this emotion not only can prevent love, but can modify its appearance in such a way as to give the impression that it has a double nature.

Love can be interpreted biologically; love can be interpreted psychologically; love can be interpreted as a cosmic force; love can be interpreted as a spiritual force, open to endless growth, and therefore not susceptible to a complete definition. We shall show that these four interpretations are intertwined. We must separate them artificially for the sake of exposition. But any one of them implies or presupposes at least two of the other three; none denies the others. No psychological interpretation of love would be possible without a biological basis; no cosmic interpretation could be attempted without a psychological perspective; and the spiritual endlessness of love is a hypothetical assumption based on premises derived from the other theories.

THE BIOLOGICAL INTERPRETATION OF LOVE

The biological interpretation of love is the one which least interests the general reader who is not versed in biology. We have already partially referred to it in Chapter 1. According to this interpretation, love is a complex of mechanisms and functions which assures the survival of the species. Sex leads to conception, pregnancy, and birth of an offspring. Survival of the newborn is guaranteed by the love of adults, generally the parents. Thus if we consider the problem only from the biological point of view of the perpetuation of the species, *love can be seen as an extension of the procreative value of sex*. Moreover, romantic love renews or revamps the sexual desire, making more probable new conceptions and new births.

Although love exists among nonhuman animals also, it does not achieve in them the expansion nor does it undergo the transformations that take place in human beings. In previous chapters we have referred to the particular circumstances of the human being, because of which he needs a much larger amount of love: the longer period of dependency of the child relative to the young of other species; the marked physical vulnerability throughout life; the psychological insecurity caused by complicated inter-personal relations; the necessity for collective actions to secure nourishment, defense, and other essentials; the more or less constant sexual desire, which is not periodic as in nonhuman animals. It is thus easy to understand why biological evolution provided not only sex, for the repro-duction of the species, but also love, for its preservation. Any human being wishes to protect his love object, no matter whether he or she is a child, a parent, an erotic partner, or a friend. In converse, we can say that love has favored evolution in certain directions because it has made it easier for the loved person to survive. The best way to favor sex and love is to make them pleasant. Thus it is not by chance that evolution has retained the association of pleasure with sex and love. There is no better way to insure reproduction and preservation of the species.

In Chapter 1 we mentioned that pleasure (sexual and possibly other types) is experienced in the septal region of the limbic system, as discovered by Olds and Milner, and possibly in other small areas of the limbic system. Love is pleasant, and therefore it must have a connection with the pleasure center or centers. But love is more than a pleasant sensation; it is an emotion. It must therefore in-volve those areas of the brain that Papez demonstrated as being responsible for emotional experience. These areas are also in the phylogenetically ancient parts of the brain and form what is now called "Papez' circle." But love also has a great deal to do with ideas, expectations, evaluations, ideals, fantasies of all sorts—psychological phenomena that, according to present knowledge, occur in phylogenet-ically recent areas of the cortex, in the parietal, occipital, temporal, and prefrontal lobes. These areas are associated with Papez' circle. Thus we may conclude that there are no love centers in the brain comparable, let us say, to the language centers, but that love is physiologically an activity of many areas of the central nervous system, which, by working together, form a functional system.

The well-known Russian neuropsychologist Aleksandr Romanovich Luria was the first one to introduce the concept of functional system, although not in relation to love or other complicated emotions, but in relation to other mental activities of the brain. Luria wrote that whereas in the first stage of development of the child a complex psychological activity rests on a more elementary basis and depends on a "basic function," in subsequent stages of development it acquires a more complex structure, that is, it becomes a functional system. This structure involves various areas of the brain, located at a distance from each other but connected by association fibers. These areas work concertedly. Although functional systems already have a complicated matrix at birth, this matrix is rudimental in comparison to the development of the organization of the system later in life. In fact, the system becomes a network of neurons which expands progressively, probably throughout life. The function of any system at a given period of time results from the concerted state of excitement and activity of many neurons and their interconnections. The various parts may be excited at the same time, or in a special sequence. A function of the system can grossly be compared to a symphony which consists of notes, some played at the same time and some in special sequences. The comparison is primitive, of course, because the musical notes are seven and the neurons are billion and their connections reach astronomical, indeterminable figures. The functional system of love is probably one of the systems which, in extension and intensity, involve more the central nervous system. We can perhaps safely say that in the experience of love, directly or indirectly, the whole brain participates. Using terms which originated with the German philosopher Nietzsche but are now of common use, we can venture the hypothesis that the more Apollonian the love, the more extended is the neocortical part of the system, and the more Dionysian the love, the larger is the limbic participation.

These very elementary neurological data show us that neurophysiologically, too, we could conceive of love as something that can increase indefinitely, as new associations can always be made among the billions of neuronal ramifications. In spite of its extremely complicated structure, the brain consumes very little physical energy. Although electric currents mediate its activities, the neuroanatomist Eccles has calculated that the whole brain operates on about ten watts. The capacity to love does not threaten to consume the available physical energy, is not like a fire which stops once the combustible material is exhausted. The flame of love is different from the flame of fire in another respect. It cannot grow in a disorganized manner. If it is an intense Dionysian love, it may seem to grow like fire, but then it may be mediated predominantly by the limbic areas, and it remains restricted. But the more involved love becomes with the spiritual, the more it departs from the original matrix. We must stress, however, that no matter how much the system of love extends in its intellectual or cognitive parts, it maintains its connections with the old brain and therefore retains a pleasant emotional tonality.

THE PSYCHOLOGICAL INTERPRETATION OF LOVE

When love is considered as a subjective experience, we interpret it psychologically. Love is no longer exclusively or predominantly a device to protect and propagate the species but something which exists for the sake of the lover, or as an end in itself. The lover experiences the pleasantness of love, and as a consequence of such experience he alters his relatedness with his love object— person, thing, or idea.

As a subjective experience, love is one of the most intense forms of experience. Consciousness, which distinguishes us from the inanimate world, puts us in a state of separateness also from other members of our species. Each of us sees, hears, touches, thinks, smells, feels; each of us is a microcosm, but we are all within our own skin, separated by our skin from the rest of the world and therefore ultimately alone. We remain so isolated unless we establish bonds with others, through communications of various kinds. That particular form of intense consciousness which is love establishes the strongest possible bond between us and our love objects. Erich Fromm was among the first to interpret love as the force with which we counterbalance our separateness. Indeed, the person who is in love does not feel alone. Even when absent, the beloved is in company with the lover, who thinks of him and longs for him. It is at the stage of the steady flow, however, that love becomes the strongest possible bond.

The previous chapters of this book have illustrated the psychological essence of the seven loves. And in each of the seven we have come to appreciate more the pleasant glow. We have also seen that except for early parental love, love cannot be compared to a gift generously given and liberally enjoyed, but to an edifice which has to be built throughout one's life with an inner law of harmony and proportion. Each human being is the architect of the edifice of his own love. We have also seen that although fear is the major obstacle to love, once love has reached the stage of steady flow, it becomes the greatest protection against fear. Since ancient times love of God has been considered the best shelter from the destructive power of fear. The Twenty-third Psalm says:

The Lord is my shepherd; I shall not want.
He maketh me to lie down in green pastures; he
   leadeth me beside the still waters.
He restoreth my soul....
I will fear no evil: for thou art with me....

Any kind of love protects us from fear, fear of others, fear of some parts of oneself, fear of aloneness and loneliness. It puts us in a state of hope of finding the green pastures or the still waters, no matter what they are for each of us. Except for love of God, the various loves do not bring about certainty, but an uncertain hope which transmutes itself not into anxiety, but into a joyful expectation. In fact, what is expected of love is already an image enwrapped by love, and thus already partially satisfying, partially alleviating the desire, as if the expected reward were to some extent already here. Thus love permits dreams, reveries, and fantasies, which become incentives to improve what we already have. Moreover, what we have already is not diminished by our desire to improve or add to it. On the other hand, the act of loving increases the value of the love object, and at the same time makes the love grow. The love object comes to be respected and at times surrounded by an aura of sacredness, especially if it is a human being, but also if it is anything significant from a human point of view.

A COSMIC INTERPRETATION OF LOVE

We have so far stressed love as a human condition or function, or as something having human significance. And yet, since we can extend the discussion of love to whatever is the object of our thoughts, feelings, and desires, in other words, potentially to the whole cosmos, can't we envision human love in a cosmic frame of reference?

According to the majority of physicists, the second principle of thermodynamics indicates that the universe is proceeding toward a slow but inevitable death. Whoever or whatever has more energy than its surroundings is in the process of losing it. For instance, if a hot object is close to an object which has a lower temperature, the warmer object loses heat while the colder acquires some, so that finally the two bodies will have the same temperature, that is, the same amount of thermal energy. The sun, too, which provides heat to our solar system, will eventually be extinguished. Compounds of organic chemistry, like petroleum or blood, lose energy by being transformed into inorganic products. Whatever is alive, or has a complicated organic structure, will eventually decompose into inorganic substances and become dust. Mountains will eventually be lowered to sea level; the amoeba will end just as a galaxy will. Whatever exists will sooner or later reach the state of simple atoms. It could even be that atoms of various elements will break and return to the original state of the simplest element, the hydrogen atom. This return to the simplest will constitute the death of the universe. This tendency toward decay, chaos, or dissolution is called by physicists entropy. Time moves only in one direction, toward increased entropy—continuously and ineluctably. People engaged in other areas of science have applied the notion of entropy to their own fields. For instance, Freud formulated the concept of the death instinct, which, according to him, exists in all of us, as a counterpart of Eros, or life instinct, and is responsible for aggression.

Other people working in scientific fields have remarked that the picture is not so gloomy. After all, centers of concentrated energy did originate; suns do exist. Moreover, at least in our planet, life came into being. Life consists of complex molecules of organic compounds that have been built up from simple inorganic compounds. Although dissolution prevails and centers of energy and living entities constitute a minimal part of the universe, they do exist. In a universe characterized mainly by entropy, antientropic, or negative entropic, forces exist, too. In an adverse physical cosmos, life emerges, survives, and evolves heroically as an antientropic, constructive force. It partially transforms the chaotic complexity of the inorganic world into the organized complexity of the biological organism. With the advent of man, the organized complexity greatly expands. No matter what adverse judgment we can pass on mankind as a whole or on its parts, we recognize in it a strong antientropic force, to be aligned with the forces that made the suns and the stars. We do not refer predominantly to man as a complex organism, as he was made, but to what he was made to make, with the three great antientropic faculties that he has at his disposal.

The first of these faculties is his reason. Because of his intellectual functions, man observes, correlates, interprets, and tries to make sense of the apparent chaos. He permanently reorganizes the world with his observations, ideas, and deeds. The increasing entropy of the world is always confronted by a permanent reorganization and reconstruction accomplished by the cognitive processes of man. Of course, the confrontation is unequal. Whatever man accomplishes is minimal in comparison to the decay of the cosmos, but very important among the sporadic constructive forces of the universe.

If the human being were endowed only with reason, he would not be as constructive as he is. He could even use his reason for destructive purposes, and as a matter of fact, he often does so. In the totality of history, however, mankind has used reason predominantly for good purposes and thus has succeeded in surviving and following a direction toward progress. Man has been able to do so because he has a second faculty which enables him to follow virtue. A feeling of oughtness, or an ethical sense, makes him select the antientropic, constructive course. Rather than follow his impulsive desires, he predominantly chooses to do the good deed, what is ultimately good for mankind. In the *Divine Comedy*, Dante has his character Ulysses remind us that we were "not made to live like animals but to follow virtue and knowledge."

However vast is the realm of man's intellect and ethics, he would not actualize his antientropic capacities as much as he can were he not motivated also by love. Virtue and knowledge, or duty and ability, are not enough. Some people may think that it is not necessary to differentiate love from virtue and postulate a third antientropic faculty. Although a right love is virtuous, we join the thinkers who distinguish love from virtue, or at least make it a special category of virtue. In fact, whereas we may follow the dictates of virtue out of a sense of duty, we follow love because we wish to do so. But of course there need be no contrast between the three faculties. As a matter of fact, *a right love is supported also by reason and virtue.*

Love is thus with us and within us, as the great promoter, the great motivational force, to provide the warmth of desire and hope, to maintain the attachment, to renew the search for more. Whatever the human being does well, he does it if moved by love—love for one's parent or child, oneself, spouse, neighbor, or fellowman, work or ideal, humanity or God. Love is the force that builds the most, that helps the most, that sustains man, who struggles to arrest or delay the Goliath of destruction. If we envision love as acting in conjunction with those antientropic physical forces that have formed stars and lives, we can then give a benevolent consideration even to the idea expressed by the ancient Greeks, Hesiod and Empedocles, that love is the force that moves things and keeps them together. What was discarded as metaphysical fantasy can be reconsidered as a concept which bridges man and the cosmos. We can thus feel at home in the universe, not because we move toward death as it does, but because we are moved by love as it is.

This cosmic love of the ancient Greeks is paralleled by Dante's last vision at the end of *Paradise*. He sees God's love as a cosmic love including all the substance which is divided and spread throughout the universe, and all the events which have visited this substance throughout the history of the world. Contrasting with the immensity and ubiquity of this love, Dante has previously told us, is the fact that God and his love are not spatial, and are therefore contained in a mathematical point deprived of dimensions.

LOVE AS ENDLESS

This Dantesque vision may be seen as one of the last feats of creativity of the great poet. It may be for us an inspiration to understand the possible lack of physicality, and thus the spirituality and the endlessness of love, even human love.

The concept of the endlessness of human love, to which we have also referred at the beginning of this chapter, can be derived from what we have shown throughout this book. Every type of love that we have examined becomes involved with an increasing number of feelings and ideas whose implications and ramifications intertwine more and more, and thus give origin to unsuspected new dimensions of feelings and understandings. It is thus impossible to define love completely, just as it is impossible completely to define man in his psychological and spiritual essence. If we define the human being as the species *Homo sapiens* in the animal kingdom, we do him a disservice, and we would be as reductionist as we are when we define love in terms only of its biological origin. For love, as it is manifested in human beings, is not primarily a physical phenomenon.

The endlessness of man is revealed also in his creativity, as one of us has described in a recent book. The possibility of systems of infinite symbolism can bring about a boundless realm of innovations. There is an important difference, however, between creativity and the experience of love. Love, although endless, brings about a feeling of fulfillment. On the other hand, even the greatest products of creativity do not make us feel absolutely satisfied, either because total knowledge is unobtainable or because our accomplishments are inferior to our ideals. Leonardo always felt dissatisfied after completing his masterpieces, which, according to him, were always short of his idealized aims. And, to return to Dante once more, in the last canto of *Paradise*—one of the most splendid passages of poetry ever written—he suffuses his verses with lyric melancholy by mentioning repeatedly how aware he is of his inadequacy at expressing the majesty of his theme, the presence of Divine Love. Dante is nevertheless able to convey to us the greatness of that love and the joy he was still feeling in remembering the final experience of his mystic journey.

Love goes far beyond being a physical phenomenon. By enabling us to understand and participate in the splendid ordering of the universe—with the promise of an endless cognitive development—love is the enemy of entropy, the friend of life and hope.

CHAPTER NOTES

PART ONE: **FIVE TYPES OF LOVE**

Chapter 1. The Rainbow of Love

Theory of approach and withdrawal
    T. C. Schneirla, pp. 1–42.
Conception of love in classical world
    Aristotle, *Metaphysics*, 1 4 984b.
    Plato, *Symposium*, 209b.
Brain as physiological organ of emotion
    J. W. Papez, pp. 725–43.
    J. Olds and P. Milner, pp. 419–27.
    P. D. MacLean, "Limbic Brain."

Chapter 2. Family Love

Causes and effects of parental love
 T. Benedek, "Psychobiology of Parenthood," pp.
  482–95.
 W. Pater, ch. 25.
 Plato, 207–8.
 E. Fromm, *Art of Loving*.
Communication of mother love to infant
 D. Schecter, pp. 264–83.
 J. Bowlby, "Child's Tie to Mother," pp. 350–73.
Development of infant's attachment to mother
 J. Bowlby, "Attachment theory," pp. 292–309;
  "Affectional bonds."
 K. Z. Lorenz.
 H. Harlow, pp. 673–85.
Infant's expectations of mother
 S. Arieti, *Interpretation of Schizophrenia*.
 W. V. Silverberg.
 M. Buber.
 E. H. Erikson.
 S. Arieti, "What is effective in the therapeutic
  process? " pp. 30–33.
Primitive organization of society and culture
 E. Morin.
Overprotection of child
 N. Shainess, "Psychological problems," pp. 46–65.
Parental fear of child's sexuality
 T. Benedek, "Psychobiology of Parenthood," pp.
  482–95.
Postpartum psychoses
 S. Arieti, "Affective disorders," pp. 449–90.
Difficulties of modern fathering
 A. Mitscherlich and M. Mitscherlich.

Effects of parental resentment of children
    I. E. Suttie.
    M. Buber.
Incest among mankind
    J. G. Flugel.

Chapter 3. Love for the Other

Difficulties of loving one's neighbor
    S. Freud.
    N. Machiavelli.
Discomfort of eye-contact
    J.-P. Sartre.

Chapter 4. Self-love

Earlier ideas of self-love
    Aristotle, *Nichomachean Ethics,* IX. 8. 1168a. 28.
    T. Aquinas, II. 11. 92b, a, h.
    M. Scheler.
Acceptance of self-love
    E. Fromm, *Man for Himself.*
Denial of Freud's view of self-love in schizophrenics
    P. Federn.
    S. Arieti, *Interpretation of Schizophrenia.*
Neurotic compensation for one's defects
    K. Horney.
Necessity of self-love
    E. Fromm, *Man for Himself.*
Concepts of identity formation
    E. H. Erikson.
    G. Lapassade.

Chapter 5. Love for Work

Functions of the creative person
   S. Arieti, *Creativity*.
Causes of exaggerated self-image
   K. Horney.

Chapter 6. Love of God

Effects of suppression of religious tendencies
   V. Frankl.
Characteristics and consequences of love of God
   E. Fromm, *Man for Himself*.
   S. Kierkegaard.

PART TWO: LOVE BETWEEN MAN AND WOMAN

Chapter 7. Erotic or Romantic Love

Psychoanalytic conceptions of love
   E. Bergler.
   W. Reich.
   H. Marcuse, *Eros and Civilization; Ideology of
      Industrial Society*.
Neo-Freudian views of love
   E. Fromm, *Art of Loving*.
   R. May.
Theories of "falling in love"
   M. Balint.
   L. Christie, pp. 244–56.

Chapter 8. The Sexual Dimension

Recent additions to knowledge of human sexuality
  W. H. Masters and V. E. Johnson.
    Human Sexual Response.
  H. S. Kaplan, *The New Sex Therapy.*
Sex centers in the brain
  P. D. MacLean, "New findings," pp. 289–301.
Clitoral and vaginal orgasms
  N. Shainess, "Feminine orgastic response."
  W. H. Masters and V. E. Johnson.
  H. S. Kaplan.
  T. Benedek, "Sexual function in women," pp. 569–91.
Causes of penis envy
  C. Thompson, "Role of women"; "Cultural pressures," p. 331.
Physiological and psychological nature of ejaculation
  A. C. Kinsey et al.
  H. S. Kaplan, personal communication.
  J. Semans, pp. 353–58.
Male impotence and related disorders
  H. S. Kaplan.
  H. I. Lief, pp. 545–68.
Sexual dissatisfactions in marriage
  E. L. Greene.
  C. J. Saeger, "Sexual dysfunctions."

Chapter 9. Equality and Inequality in the Love Relation

Masculine and feminine roles
  E. Maccoby and N. J. Jacklin.

Opposing views of homogamy
> L. G. Burchinan.
> R. F. Winch, pp. 552–55.

Johnson's opinion of the inevitability of dominance
> J. Boswell, *Life of Johnson*.

Psychological and political suppression of women
> H. Deutsch. The only woman ever chosen a member of the ruling inner circle of the Soviet Communist Party was the late Yacaterina Furtseva, according to the *New York Times*, 25 Oct. 1974.
> H.Lerner, pp. 538–53.

Example of absurdity of some time-hallowed practices
> Cro-Magnon men, who lived probably between 10,000 and 80,000 years ago, identified red powder with blood and therefore with life. They sprinkled the corpses of relatives with ochre in hope that this color would restore them to life. From evidence at different excavations, this practice seems to have persisted for at least 20,000 years, long after everyone should have been convinced of its futility.

Female suppression of women
> R. Moulton, "Sexual conflicts."

Female depression in marriage
> S. Arieti, "Approach to depression," pp. 397–406; "Affective disorders," pp. 449–90.

Chapter 10. Living Together and Its Common Vicissitudes

Faulty mutual cueing
> M. Mahler.

Chapter 11. Marriages in Trouble

Chapter 12. Love's Expectations

PART THREE: **LOVE OF LIFE AND A THEORY OF LOVE**

Chapter 13. Love of Life

Lack of love of life
    A. Schopenhauer, *World as Will and Idea*; "Vanity
    of existence."
    C. Darrow, as quoted by A. Weinberg.

Chapter 14. A Theory of Love

Theories of biological origins of love
    J. Olds and P. Milner, pp. 419–27.
    J. W. Papez, pp. 725–43.
    A. R. Luria, *Cortical Function; Working Brain*.
    J. C. Eccles, pp. 135–146.
Cosmic interpretation of love
    Dante, *Inferno*, Canto XXVI, vv. 119–20; *Paradise*,
        Canto XXXIII, vv. 85–90; *Paradise*, Canto XXVIII,
        vv. 16–45.
Endlessness of man
    S. Arieti, *Creativity*, ch. 18.

SOURCES

Aquinas, Thomas. *Summa Theologica*.

Arieti, S. "What Is Effective in the Therapeutic Process?" *American Journal of Psychoanalysis* 17 (1957):30–33.

———. "The Psychotherapeutic Approach to Depression." *American Journal of Psychotherapy* 16 (1962): 397–406.

———. *Interpretation of Schizophrenia*. New York: Basic Books, 1974.

———, ed. "Affective Disorders: Manic-Depressive Psychosis and Psychotic Depression." In *American Handbook of Psychiatry*, edited by S. Arieti, 2nd ed. 3:449–90. New York: Basic Books, 1974.

———. *Creativity: The Magic Synthesis*. New York: basic Books, 1976.

Aristotle. *Metaphysics*.

————. *Nichomachean Ethics.*

Balint, M. *Primary Love and Psychoanalytic Technique.* London: Tavistock, 1965.

Benedek, T. "Sexual Functions in Women and Their Disturbances." In *American Handbook of Psychiatry,* edited by S. Arieti, 2d ed. 1:569–91. New York: Basic Books, 1974.

————. "The Psychobiology of Parenthood." In *American Handbook of Psychiatry,* edited by S. Arieti. 2d ed. 1:482–95. New York: Basic Books, 1974.

Bergler, E. *Unhappy Marriage and Divorce.* New York: International Universities Press, 1946.

Black, P. *Physiological Correlates of Emotion.* New York: Academic Press, 1970.

Boswell, James. *Life of Johnson.*

Bowlby, J. "The Nature of the Child's Tie to His Mother." *International Journal of Psychoanalysis* 39 (1958): 350–73.

————. "Affectional Bonds: Their Nature and Origin." In *Loneliness,* edited by R. S. Weiss. Cambridge: M.I.T. Press, 1973.

————. "Attachment Theory, Separation Anxiety, and Mourning." In *American Handbook of Psychiatry,* edited by S. Arieti. 2d ed. 6:292–309. New York: Basic Books, 1974.

Buber, M. *I and Thou.* Edinburgh: Clark, 1953.

Burchinan, L. G. "The Premarital Dyad and Love Involvement." In *Handbook of Marriage and the Family,* edited by H. T. Christensen. Chicago: Rand McNally, 1964.

Christie, L. "The Origins of Falling in Love and Infatuation." *American Journal of Psychotherapy* 26 (1972):244–56.

Dante. *Inferno.* Canto XXVI.

————. *Paradise. Canto XXVIII; Canto XXXIII.*

Deutsch, H. *Psychology of Women*. New York: Grune & Stratton, 1945.

Eccles, J. C. "The Physiology of Imagination." *Scientific American* 199 (1958):3, 135–46.

Erikson, E. H. *Childhood and Society*. New York: Norton, 1950.

Federn, P. *Ego Psychology and the Psychoses*. New York: Basic Books, 1952.

Flugel, J. C. *The Psychoanalytic Study of the Family*. London: Hogarth Press, 1926.

Frankl, V. *The Unconscious God*. New York: Simon & Schuster, 1975.

Freud, S. *Civilization and Its Discontents*. London: Hogarth Press, 1946.

Fromm, E. *Man for Himself*. New York: Rinehart, 1947.

———. *The Art of Loving*. New York: Harper, 1956.

Greene, B. L. *A Clinical Approach to Marital Problems: Evaluation and Management*. Springfield, Ill.: Charles C. Thomas, 1970.

Harlow, H. "The Nature of Love." *American Psychology* 13 (1958):673–85.

Horney, Karen. *Neurosis and Human Growth*. New York: Norton, 1950.

Kaplan, H. S. *The New Sex Therapy*. New York: Brunner-Mazel, 1974.

Kierkegaard, S. *Fear and Trembling*. Garden City, N.Y.: Doubleday Anchor Books, 1954.

Kinsey, A. C.; Pomeroy, W. B.; and Martin, C. E. *Sexual Behavior in the Human Male*. Philadelphia: W. B. Saunders, 1948.

Lapassade, G. *L'Entrée dans la vie*. Paris: De Minuit, 1963.

Lerner, H. "Early Origins of Envy and Devaluation in Women: Implications for Sex Role Stereotypes." *Bulletin of the Menninger Clinic* 37 (1973):538–53.

Lief, H. I. "Sexual Functions in Men and Their Disturbances." In *American Handbook of Psychiatry*, edited by S. Arieti. 2d ed. 1:545–68. New York: Basic Books, 1974.

Lorenz, K. Z. *"Der Kupman in der Umvelt des Vogels."* *J. Orn. Berl.* 83 (1935). Translated in *Instinctive Behavior.* New York: International. Universities Press, 1957.

Luria, A. R. *Higher Cortical Functions in Man.* New York: Basic Books, 1966.

————. *The Working Brain. An Introduction to Neuropsychology.* New York: Basic Books, 1973.

Maccoby, E. and Jacklin, N. J. *The Psychology of Sex Differences.* Stanford, Calif.: Stanford University Press, 1974.

Machiavelli, N. *The Prince.*

MacLean, P. D. "New Findings Relevant to the Evolution of Psychosexual Functions of the Brain." *Journal of Nervous and Mental Disease* 135 (1962):289–301.

————. "The Limbic Brain in Relation to the Psychoses." In *Physiological Correlates of Emotion,* edited by P. Black. New York: Academic Press, 1970.

Mahler, M. "On Human Symbiosis and the Vicissitudes of Individuation." *Infantile Psychosis.* New York: International Universities Press, 1968.

Marcuse, H. *Eros and Civilization: A Philosophical Inquiry into Freud.* Boston: Beacon, 1955.

————. *One-Dimensional Man: Studies in the Ideology of Advanced Industrial Society.* Boston: Beacon, 1964.

Masters, W. H. and Johnson, V. E. *Human Sexual Response.* Boston: Little, Brown, 1966.

May, Rollo. *Love and Will.* New York: Norton, 1969.

Mitscherlich, A. and Mitscherlich, M. "Fathers and Fatherhood in Our Time." *The World Biennial of Psychiatry and Psychotherapy,* edited by S. Arieti. Vol. 2. New York: Basic Books, 1973.

Morin, E. *Le Paradigme perdu: la nature humaine.* Paris: Editions du Seuil, 1973.

Moulton, Ruth. "Sexual Conflicts of Contemporary Women." *Interpersonal Explorations in Psychoanalysis,* edited by E. Witenberg. New York: Basic Books, 1973.

The New York Times. 26 October 1974.

Olds, J. and Milner, P. "Positive Reinforcement Produced by Electrical Stimulation of Septal Area and Other Regions of Rat Brain." *Journal of Comparative and Physiological Psychology* 47 (1954):419–27.

Papez, J. W. "A Proposed Mechanism of Emotion." *Archives of Neurology and Psychiatry 37* (1937): 725–43.

Pater, W. *Marius the Epicurean.* New York, 1885.

Plato. *Symposium.*

Reich, Wilhelm. *Character Analysis.* New York: Orgone Institute Press, 1949.

Sager, C. J. "Sexual Dysfunctions and Marital Discord." In H. S. Kaplan, *The New Sex Therapy.* New York: Brunner-Mazel, 1974.

Sartre, J.-P. *Being and Nothingness.* New York: Citadel Press, 1969.

Schecter, D. "Infant Development." In *American Handbook of Psychiatry,* edited by S. Arieti, 2d ed. 1: 264–83. New York: Basic Books, 1974.

Scheler, M. *Sympathetic II.*

Schneirla, T. C. "An Evolutionary and Developmental Theory of Biphasic Processes Underlying Approach and Withdrawal." *Nebraska Symposium on Motivation.* Pp. 1–42. Lincoln: University of Nebraska Press, 1959.

Schopenhauer, A. *The World As Will and Idea.* Vol. 3.

———. "The Vanity of Existence." In *The Will to Live: Selected Writings of Arthur Schopenhauer,* edited by Richard Taylor. New York, 1962.

Semans, J. "Premature Ejaculation, A New Approach." *Southern Medical Journal* 44 (1956):353–58.

Shainess, N. "Psychological Problems Associated with Motherhood." In *American Handbook of Psychiatry,* edited by S. Arieti, 1st ed. 3:46–65. New York: Basic Books, 1966.

―――. "Authentic Feminine Orgastic Response." In *Sexuality and Psychoanalysis,* edited by E. Adelson. New York: Brunner-Mazel, 1975.

Silverberg, W. V. *Childhood Experience and Personal Destiny.* New York: Springer, 1952.

Suttie, I. E. *The Origins of Love and Hate.* New York: Julian Press, 1952.

Thompson, C. "The Role of Women in This Culture." *Psychiatry* 4 (1941):1.

―――. "Cultural Pressures in the Psychology of Women." *Psychiatry* 5 (1942):331.

Weinberg, A. *Clarence Darrow—Attorney for the Damned.* New York: Simon & Schuster, 1957.

Winch, R. R. "The Theory of Complementary Needs in Mate-Selection; Final Results on the Test of General Hypotheses." *American Sociological Review* 20 (1955):552–55.

INDEX

Abraham, 87–88
absolute, seeking the, see God, love of
accomplishment, 69, 73
Adler, Alfred, 76
Aeneid (Virgil), 13, 91
aggression, 55, 169
Albee, Edward, 172
alcohol, 53
ambitious marriages, 165–66, 167
anger, 15, 55
animals, sex drive of, 93–94, 119
Anna Karenina (Tolstoy), 192
anxiety, 15, 33, 52
Appollonian-Dionysian love, 203
approach and withdrawals, 3, 52–53, 92
Aquinas, Thomas, 59
Arieti, S., 26, 31, 48
Aristotle, 9, 45–46, 58–59, 80

attachment, 23–25
  "anxious," 35
authority, 46–47

baby, see infant
Bachofen, 97
beauty, 181–82
Beckett, Samuel, 178
belonging, love of work and, 69–70
Benedek, Therese, 18, 19, 123
Bergler, Edmund, 96
biological interpretation of love, 200–3
Bowlby, John, 22, 23–25, 35
Buber, Martin, 33, 135

child's love, see also father; mother, 23–29
  attachment and, 23–25